GANG-GANG SARAH:
A CARIBBEAN SENSATION

By

R OSELLE T HOMPSON

EAGLE PUBLICATIONS

Published by Eagle Publications
P O Box 73374, London W3 3FZ, England.
A Paperback Original

First published in the United Kingdom in 2020

Text copyright © 2020 Roselle Thompson

The right of Roselle Thompson to be identified as the Author of this work has been asserted by her.

ISBN 978-1-8381068-3-6

A CIP catalogue record for this book is available from the British Library
All Rights Reserved
This book is sold subject to the condition that it shall not, by way of trade or otherwise, be lent, hired out or otherwise circulated in any form of binding or cover other than that in which it is published. No part of this publication may be reproduced, stored in a retrieval system, or transmitted in any form or by any means (electronic, mechanical, photocopying, recording or otherwise) without the prior written permission of Eagle Publications.

All paper used by Eagle Publications is SFI (Sustainable Forestry Initiative) and PEFC (Programme for the Endorsement of Forest Certification Schemes) Certified.
This is a work of fiction. Names, characters, incidents and dialogues are products of the author's imagination or are used fictitiously. Any resemblance to actual people, living or dead, events or locales is entirely coincidental.

Printed in the United Kingdom and United States by Lightning Source for Eagle Publishers

www.eaglepublications.org.uk

CONTENTS

Introduction	**1**
Notes to the Introduction	**32**
Characters	**38**
Act 1 Sc. 1: Welcome to the Caribbean!	39
Act 1 Sc. 2: Kidnap Raids	43
Act 1 Sc. 3: The Conspiracy	47
Act 1 Sc. 4: Naming Ceremony Interrupted	50
Act 1 Sc. 5: The Prophecy	54
Act 2 Sc. 1: Stolen Children Leave Africa	57
Act 2 Sc. 2: Middle Passage Crossing Lament	60
Act 3 Sc. 1: Arrival Day in the Caribbean	63
Act 3 Sc. 2: First Day Plantation Woes	65
Act 3 Sc. 3: Gang-Gang's Recovery	70
Act 3 Sc. 4: Rise to Prominence	72
Act 3 Sc. 5: The Birth Attendant	75
Act 4 Sc. 1: Dinner Boasts	79
Act 4 Sc. 2: The Cane Work-Song	84
Act 4 Sc. 3: Christianising Ade	87
Act 4 Sc.4: Pass it on! - *The Kalinda*	91
Act 4 Sc. 5: Obeah man & The Silk Cotton Tree	95
Act 4 Sc. 6: Karmic Effect in the Great House	98
Act 4 Sc. 7: Moral & Spiritual Dilemmas	103
Act 5 Sc. 1: Gang-Gang's Reward: A Name	109
Act 5 Sc. 2: Appeasing Papa Bois	113
Act 5 Sc. 3: Wedding & Rebellion Plans	118
Act 5 Sc. 4: Divided Loyalties	123
Act 5 Sc. 5: Jabari Calls for Revolution	127
Act 5 Sc. 6: Secret Rebellion Plans	133
Act 5 Sc. 7: Cry Freedom! *Jumping the Broomstick*	138
Epilogue	**143**
Glossary	**144**

INTRODUCTION

This play is a work of fiction, based on a story depicting Gang-Gang Sarah, who Tobagonian and Trinidadian Folktales claim, was an African woman who 'flew' from West Africa to Tobago), in order to take care of her people spiritually, on Plantations during Slavery in the region. Therefore, having such a socio-historical and cultural importance ought to have signposted Gang-Gang Sarah as a person of great prominence, given her role of enabling the survival of African slaves; who overcame kidnap in Africa, survival of the treacherous Transatlantic crossing on board Slave Ships, and ended up in Tobago.

Added to such leadership qualities, the folktale claims that Gang-Gang Sarah was 'a witch,' with supernatural powers, as well as a plantation mid-wife or *Doula*. It is said that she was known by everyone in Les Couteaux in Tobago, where she finally settled and died. Legend also states that she became the wife of someone called Tom, whom she had known previously in West Africa, when they were children and whom she later married. Once slaves were freed, the folktale states that Gang-Gang Sarah tried to 'fly back to Africa' but was unable to do so, as she had broken witchcraft rules about eating salt, which resulted in her losing the power to fly! Consequently, the legend states that being unable to fly off from the silk cotton tree, Gang-Gang Sarah fell and died.

Today, there is a marked silk cotton tree in Tobago, (known throughout the Caribbean as either *god tree, devil tree,* or *jumbie tree),* where Gang-Gang Sarah was supposed to have fallen from, and an obscured burial spot in Tobago. These are all that appears to exist as a record about this warrior of revolutionary proportions; a perfunctory note, of what is clearly an overlooked Caribbean icon, who should be acknowledged. There is a lack of detailed attention paid to this female legend, whose resistant and healing roles in both slavery and post-slavery periods, should have been given greater prominence, in the island's/region's historical data.

Arguably, more attention seems to have been paid to the silk cotton tree and its cultural significance, compared to the linkages and enormity of the roles played by Gang-Gang Sarah.

From one perspective, Gang-Gang Sarah's fragmented history, conversely, seems to highlight her importance as a Caribbean slave woman who had specific qualities to resist slavery during colonisation. She seemed to have functioned as a lead female, in preserving both the African people and their culture in the Caribbean region. Therefore, acknowledging Gang-Gang Sarah's socio-historical, cultural, and political importance, squared against the lack of recorded data, led to further research into similar documented historical female roles in the Caribbean region, during slavery. Findings revealed a paucity of salient information in this regard, except for Jamaican Nanny, who it seems, is the only documented Caribbean female of note, during slavery in the English-speaking Caribbean; this is in comparison to the well-documented male revolutionaries in the region during the same period. Consequently, it would seem that the history of female revolutionaries during the era of slavery has been neglected, and in telling the story of Gang-Gang Sarah, a seminal figure connecting the Caribbean and West Africa, the play helps to remedy this, by providing a depiction of many aspects of the Afro-Caribbean experience, viz enslavement in Africa, The Middle Passage crossing and plantation life.

Re-evaluating the trope: From '*witch*' to *warrior* woman

Exploring Gang-Gang Sara's character further revealed how possible linkages of her role in the Tobagonian/Caribbean legend, can be equated with the tradition of African women warriors; a fact which highlights the antecedents of an African tradition, where women, once referred to as Dahomey Amazons, from West Africa, (part of contemporary Benin), were an all-female military, with a protective and, initially, a hunting role. They were known as *gbeto* or keepers of the tribe, and were later comprised of the Dahomean

King's wives, known as *ahosi,* as well as slaves from conquests in neighbouring villages and tribes. These women were fierce warriors who underwent intense training in survival skills; often in hand-to-hand combat amongst themselves. Their rigorous roles rendered them almost impervious to pain with an indifferent attitude to death; seen in their rigorous initiation tests and training. These all-female warriors armed with muskets, operated as bodyguards and militia, in order to defeat neighbouring kingdoms.

    Therefore, an interesting connection can be made between (Gang-Gang Sarah), the African warrior woman, who was sent to the Caribbean to look after the slaves but was branded "a witch who could fly," is perhaps in keeping with a misconceived image of this African woman warrior's acrobatic and military prowess, as opposed to literally flying. Furthermore, Gang-Gang Sarah's role in the Caribbean can be compared to African women warriors who were *keepers of the tribe*; those who also have the authority to take over and construct/reconstruct society.

Interestingly, the legend of Gang-Gang Sarah in Tobago, also resonates with the story of Nanny of Jamaica, the 18th century leader of the Jamaican Maroons, who led a community of formerly enslaved Africans to victory against British colonisers. Nanny was also reputed to be "a witch" who legend claims, could bounce bullets off her backside and target them back to her colonial assailants. Contrary to the negativity of this portrayal, *Nanny of Jamaica*, or *Queen Nanny, Granny Nanny* or just *Nanny,* has been fully recognised as a Jamaican national heroine of immense importance in the history of Jamaica.

Today, the subject of the African woman warrior's role has again been given prominence, thanks to the 2018 Oscar-winning blockbuster Hollywood movie**, Black Panther**, which presented remarkable military and combative skills from an all-female army called the Dora Milaje, in Wakanda, a fictional African futurist country. In fact, a real-life equivalent of the Dora Milaje, the [1]***Agoji*** warriors, exist in present day Benin, (formerly the kingdom of Dahomey), and is said to have had trade links with European slavers during the reign of the third King of Dahomey, King Houegbadja, (1645 – 1685), who created the first women warriors. Given Gang-Gang's original background, linked to her role as an African woman warrior, there is need for a re-evaluation of perspectives concerning Gang-Gang Sarah, the Caribbean slave who, arguably, was originally an African woman warrior, who subsequently applied her warrior traits in the Caribbean environment but these were misconstrued as being supernatural and labelled as witchcraft. Furthermore, given the contesting dominance of the European religious beliefs on slave plantations during this time, it is possible to conclude that labelling Gang-Gang Sarah "a witch," served Christian ideology of debunking African religious practices, rather than accepting Gang-Gang Sarah's traditional warrior's role. The fact is, branding Gang-Gang Sarah as "a witch," has negative connotations, associated with a person, especially a woman, who is supposed to practice magic or sorcery with the aid of the devil, and this would have been contrary to the dominant Christian beliefs in the region at that time. Such a label would have downgraded Gang-Gang Sarah's cultural importance in the environment, thereby obfuscating and debunking her level of importance in the colonised Caribbean.

Therefore, it is possible that re-evaluating the trope would help to clarify the anomaly between branding Gang-Gang Sarah as "a *witch,*" vis-à-vis positively reinstating and locating her Caribbean role, in West African antecedent. In Act 3, when Gang-Gang Sarah topples the Slave Manager from his horse, the skill and affront she used to do so, shocked and frightened the other slaves, confirms her specialist, professional training. Also towards the end of the Play in Act 5, Gang-Gang is seen instructing the women warriors whom she had been secretly training as a female militia, on the plantation, with protective and combative roles. The play suggests they, would be able to lead with authority and assist in reconstructing society, in their post-rebellion stage.

This play's exploratory timeline begins with Gang-Gang Sarah's experiences, which commence with being raided and traded on the African continent with others, their Transatlantic crossing, colonisation, slavery, and plantation settlement in the Tobago/Caribbean, to the mid-19th century. This timeline makes it a tale of epic proportions, since it simultaneously presents other reading perspectives, and sub-stories, which date from 15th and 16th centuries to mid-19th century. It is a period that encompassed the lives of raided African people, their subjugated lives on plantations as slaves, rebellion, emancipation, and post-emancipation periods. Overall, the play showcases Gang-Gang Sarah's story as the frame story or main narrative, that leads the reader from this first story, to several emergent sub-plays within the play, whilst highlighting myriad thematic concerns in them. For example, the main frame-story about Gang-Gang Sarah's life, appears to open up a window on the following:

- The *story of Anancy* in the Caribbean. Anancy's story is encapsulated in the main narrative, forming the [2]***mise-en-abime***, with signifiers within the text that lead to other narratives.
- The story narrates *historiocity of the Slave Triangle and colonisation.*
- Highlights the *making of the Caribbean* with its trading route that began in Africa to the Caribbean, then to England, and back again to Africa.
- *Slavery in the Caribbean* (as a main theme), is presented in the frame story.
- African complicity in the slave trade which enabled *slave capture and trading.*
- The *development and expansion of the Sugar Plantation* in the Caribbean.
- The influence, growth and development of *African religious and spiritual beliefs in the Caribbean.*
- The politics of *male dis-empowerment and the matrifocal family.*
- The possible role of *transplantation, acculturation and synthesism of African cultures* in the Caribbean.

However, although this play focuses solely on the African slaves' input into the Caribbean, it is important to state categorically, that the very first peoples of this twin-island republic – Trinidad and Tobago - included Amerindian tribes, often described as Caribs and Arawaks, from as early as 8000BC. These indigenous peoples had lived there for centuries, evolving their own civilisation, travelling inter-island, often moving from Tobago to mainland Trinidad; where they traded, in hunting dogs, hammocks, and parrots. In other words, the African slaves were not the first islanders. However, it is widely known that many of the Caribs and Arawaks throughout the Caribbean region, resisted colonisation; many died of diseases from contact with the European intruders, some fought colonisers, others chose to kill themselves, rather than be caught and forced into slavery; thereby drastically depleting their numbers. In 1592, The Amerindian population of Trinidad and Tobago was numbered at around 40,000; by 1634, this number had been drastically reduced to only 4,000. Today, the government of Trinidad and Tobago continues to intensify its efforts to promote and support recovery of the indigenous heritage. The Santa Rosa Carib Community is the last remaining organized group of people identifying with an Amerindian identity and way of life, approximating some 12,000 people in Northeast Trinidad.[3]

The most common groups of enslaved Africans in Trinidad and Tobago were [4]*Igbo* (also known as Ibo**)**, [5]*Congo*, [6]*Ibibio* and [7]*Malinke* people, mainly from West and Central Africa, who became the largest ethnic group in Trinidad and Tobago. In 1498 Christopher Columbus landed in Trinidad, and the island soon became a territory of the Spanish Empire. However, by 1517 the Spanish slave owners and their administrators had mixed with the slave population, thus creating offspring that were known as *Mulattos*; a Spanish-derived term, used to describe people of mixed black and white ancestry.

Adding to the general mixed cultural environment, in 1783, the Spanish King (Jose de Galvez) passed a **law**[8] which promised free land to Europeans who were willing to relocate to Trinidad to work. As a result, French settlers migrated to Trinidad from nearby Grenada, (a French colony at the time), and the French Antilles, to work on sugar cane plantations; thus, creating a [9]**Creole** identity, (a person of black decent and mixed European e.g., Spanish and French), in the mixed ancestry of Trinidadians. However, such was the fierce pursuit and competition between European countries to conquer other lands, Britain gained Trinidad from Spain via the Treaty of Amiens, in 1802. Later in 1834, with the abolition of slavery, a further influx of migrants, Indian indentured labourers, with their own varieties of languages were brought in by the British, to work in the island. This was followed by European indentured servants, including French, Spanish, Germans, Swiss, Portuguese, British (e.g., Irish, Scottish, and Welsh), Italians and Dutch. Much later, Chinese, Lebanese, Arabs, Norwegians, Mexicans, and Polish people - all joined Trinidad & Tobago's culturally diverse environment.

Language issues in the Play

As with the racial and cultural input discussed above, another manifestation of cultural diversity is the mixture of languages in the island. At the start of the Play, an attempt is made by Anancy, to highlight the polylingual nature of the environment, shown by her varied welcome address to the audience, acknowledging its rich mixture of languages. In other words, despite being in the same environment, there is a noticeable variation in the forms, styles, and expressions of language uttered by the characters. As a result, a similar process of transformation took place in the languages of the people. This is because the different input of peoples' languages in the Caribbean, resulted in a synthesis of languages, so that far from being a single spoken Caribbean language, there were several permutations of speech that created what is characteristically known as Creole language. In the English-speaking Caribbean, a Creole language is identified by its combination of African syntax and European lexicon or words. This view was confirmed, over a century and a half ago, by J.J. Thomas, whose definition of the Creole language, in his *Theory and Practice of Creole Grammar* (1869) is, "a dialect framed by Africans from a European tongue."[10] Such perspectives are based on the largest proportion of racial groups or speakers forming the population.

Today, Scholars agree that the written forms of the English language, in the former and current British-controlled Caribbean countries, conform to the spelling and the grammatical styles of Britain.

We can agree that given the forced contact of outsiders into the Caribbean region onto the indigenous Amerindians, [11](*Caribs and Arawaks* and in some regions *Tainos*), their language was impacted on by varieties of spoken languages of the slaves from West and Central Africa. Many of these slaves were literate in their own native languages and not being from one single area in Africa, spoke different tribal dialects, were forced to speak the European colonisers' languages, (e.g., English, French, Dutch, Spanish), in the region.

At the start of the play, Act 1 Sc. 1, Anancy introduces herself to the audience, as *Mrs. Anancy*, and makes it clear that she has a limitless licence to use *any* language register; "including Twi, Ga, Fanti, Yoruba, Creole, French Patois, Nation Language, the European languages, as well as Chinese and Japanese" – in both their standard and non-standard forms! (Act 1 Sc.1). With this seemingly bold assertion, Anancy is claiming the right to interject in any form, and any time, depending on the situation her choice of response merits, showing her adaptability to them. The language issue implies that symbolically, she has adapted and resisted superpower linguistic domination in the region, when she claims the authority to speak as one who has inherited a polylingual background. Specifically, she attributes this to interactions with the languages of slave owners, slave handlers or managers, overseers; (in the case of the British colonisers, they brought different variations of English; from Irish, Welsh, and English speakers). Added to this situation, in the 1800s, were Indian languages from India, whose own varieties and expressions were added to the environment; thus, expanding the fusion and variations of the Creole language.

It is important to note that this language evolved out of the necessity to communicate in a common language for survival on the plantations. Consequently, individual islands within the whole region, tend to have a European language dominance, due to the influence of their ruling colonial power, over periods of time. Historically, colonisers had fought for control of individual islands; seizing, and losing them at different times, so that their diverse histories are also reflected in the spoken languages of the people.

Additionally, when Anancy mentions Chinese and Japanese influence, there is a sense that she is expanding the international sphere of influence that Caribbean folklore enjoys. At the same time, she draws attention to the Caribbean languages which, in the play, have different styles. This can be based on the age of the person speaking, and the closeness of interacting with European speakers, since formal education was an impossibility. For example, Edith and Ade's spoken language is presented as being closer to Standard English, because of their close working environment, as House Slaves, to the Plantation Owner and his family. This is compared to the elder slaves, who lived only among the plantation slaves, and whose style of speaking show a shortened version of English, with different forms of English utterances. Noticeable language features used among the characters of this play, are presented in Caribbean English, as follows:

1. **Different sets of pronouns** are used to alter the slaves English language utterance, **e.g. *mi*= for my; *ah* = for I; *all-you* = all of you; *dem* = them; *deh* = that; *dat* = there; *dis* = this.**

2. **Consonant changes** in the slaves' speech, like dropping **th,** or the **g** in present continuous verb tenses, are also common. E.g. *"Well yes, dey say Ol' Joe pass out two littl' stones, all de way from his kidneys, by drinkin' medicine from de tree; leaves, bark and flowers – everythin'. (Act 4 Sc.5).*

3. **Repetition** helps to conveys a sense of immediacy. For example, the 1st Canecutter who visits the Obeah man shows his fear when he says: (Act 4 Sc. 5); *Yes sah! Hurry! Hurry! sah!* Another example is, *"So is 'fraid, I 'fraid oh! 'Cause ah no go cut down no tree, Baba!"* (Act 4 Sc.5).

4. A noticeable *interchange of first pronoun*, such as **ah** and *I* in the same sentence; used for emphasis, together with the double negative use of *"no go cut down no tree"* – instead of, *"*I'm not going to cut down any tree," in the same sentence.

5. **Word-order,** accompanied by the tone of voice for emphasis, generally adds meaning to the utterance. Here is a general example found in the Caribbean: *"Wey the bwoy iz?"* = Where is the boy? *Wey dat bwoy dey?* = Where is that boy?

   Likewise, Anancy in Act 4 Sc.3 says: *"All-you better watch out too, eh!"* and *"All-you doh joke with our silk cotton tree, eh!"*

6. **Inconsistency in past-tense and plural forms** – In Act 4 Sc. 7, Edith says to Gang-Gang Sarah, "Ma-ma, you mus' come quick! Massah children, dey dying, bring medicine now!"

In the Caribbean today, the above examples will vary further, based on whether the speaker is from a **rural or urban area,** or whether the language is uttered by an **Afro-** or **Indo-**descent speaker. However, the language issue is a complex one, and in Act I Sc. 1, when Anancy first greets the audience, she addresses them jokingly with a series of language varieties that reflect the language complexity in the region. Mrs Anancy's forms of greeting make the theme of language a first consideration for the audience. Notice how the fusion of language and its influence is subtly alluded to, as follows:

1. *"How-de-doo! How-de-doo!* (a variety of Creole English - the speech pattern of the older generation).
2. *"Welcome!"* (Standard English greeting)
3. *"E Kaaro o!"* (West African, Nigerian greeting)
4. *Wha' happenin' deh?"* (Creole English greeting)
5. *"Que passa?"* (Spanish greeting)

6. Anancy adds a further input from the French colonials when she calls the audience's attention to the French-based Creole language with *"Bonswar"* instead of *"Bon soir,"* meaning good night, in Standard French. Today, this type of vernacular is spoken in Dominica, Grenada, St. Lucia, St. Martin, St. Vincent and the Grenadines.

7. Anancy then deliberately adds a Standard French greeting, *"Bon jour"* meaning "Good day/morning"; which is the official spoken language in some Caribbean islands such as Guadeloupe, Haiti, Martinique, Barthelemy and St. Martin.

8. Finally, bringing more modern forms of greeting found in the region, she asks the audience if they would prefer to be addressed in Americanism, prevalent in modern Caribbean language versions; *"How you guys doing?"* or *"What's up?"*

Therefore, Anancy's tactical opening gambit alludes to the language transformation in the traumatised environment, to its present-day versions, aims to show that we are not dealing with a homogenous group with a single spoken language. The fact is, the Creole languages, over 500 years old, have been wrongly classified as dialects of English and French. Co-existing as it does alongside Standard English, Caribbean language varieties have been stigmatised because they are linked to slavery, poverty, backwardness, or lack of education, and those on the lower socio-economic levels in society. In fact, this issue presented in Caribbean works of art, for over 90 years, has been the subject of debates among scholars and writers within and outside of the region, who have debated whether to use Standard English for ease of access to a wider, global audience, or in limiting this to a parochial audience, insist on endorsing the legitimacy of Creole varieties in their texts. Similarly, it is hoped that the issue of language presented in this play will add to current debates, whilst highlighting the ability and skilfulness of Caribbean speakers to switch between Creole and Standard English, (or somewhere between the two), as well as other developed forms of expressions. Consequently, it adds to debates on Caribbean languages' right to be identified, recognised, and studied as Standard forms, and not as dialects of other languages.

Folklore

❖ **Anancy**

Perhaps one of the most dominant features in the play is seen in the process through which African people, who were shipped to the Caribbean region as slaves, and their succeeding generations who were born in the region, became Caribbean people. Therefore, through specific character portrayal, there are fictionally presented scenarios that suggest how African culture may have been synthesised and became the mainstay of cultural and religious practices in the Caribbean. For example, the significance of Anancy, the play's narrator, is also the story of how [12]***Anancy, Brer Anancy, Anansi, Ananse* or *Mrs. Anancy*,** found its way into Caribbean culture and folklore.

In West African folklore, the original *Ananse* is an Akan god, who knows and sees everything; an omniscient and omnipotent sky god in the Akan language; considered to be the spirit of all knowledge. Though slightly transformed, in the Caribbean environment, he is the teller of the tales who transmits the stories, as one who has all knowledge of stories but due to the role he plays in the Caribbean environment, he becomes a trickster figure, whose aim is to help the slaves outwit their slave-master through cunning. Therefore, as a Caribbean icon, the 'transformed Anancy' can be said to be 'born' in the new environment. Traditionally, in the folklore, Anancy's gender is male. His survival in the Caribbean and his cunning ways also symbolise resistance to powerful slave owners and colonialism. Therefore, in this play, Anancy is presented as an elder, in [13]***crick-crack*** fashion, passing down knowledge and moral messages to the younger generations and audiences, through its narration. As such, Anancy is given licence to speak with authority, on all issues, via various interventions throughout the scenes of the play. However, in this play, there is one major difference - a traditional shift; instead of being a male, Anancy is characterised as a female character.

Notwithstanding this, in Act 3, Anancy claims to also be the slaves' state of mind, their cunning, and is instrumental in their retention of African traditions. It is possible to see how this elderly repository of oral storytelling, from the transformations that she has personally undergone, demonstrate the way African identities have travelled and were renewed in the Caribbean. Anancy makes it clear at the end of the Act 3 Sc 1, when the slaves arrived in Tobago, *"It's a place where from today, I'm no longer Akan Ananse, but become Anancy the spider, a trickster in the Caribbean; among them I will hide, tasked with this new role, to lead and guide, as directed by Olodumare."* In other words, Anancy, who has witnessed the slave crossing, is a reliable eyewitness of the events that surround the slaves from Africa, on board the Slave ships, and their lives in their Caribbean location. In effect, Mrs Anancy becomes an Akan folktale character, who bridges the gap between the African people *before* and *after* they became slaves, in the synthesized nature of their new environment.

- ❖ **Papa Bois**

Another folkloric icon in the play is [14]***Papa Bois***. Papa Bois is also *Maitre Bois* (master of the woods), in areas where Creole is spoken, (St. Lucia, Dominica, Guadeloupe, Grenada, Martinique) and called *Daddy Bouchon* (hairy man), in other areas. But the name is French originated and translated means *(Father of the Woods*), suggesting that this tale in the Caribbean may have stemmed from French-Creole speaking Africans and French colonists who were permitted to settle in the Spanish-owned Trinidad, by a Cedula instigated by a French Planter, P. R. Roume de Saint Laurent, from neighbouring Grenada; a French colony (1694-1763).

In the Caribbean, as was the practice in Africa, Papa Bois must be appeased before the forest could be disturbed, and even so, those wishing to avail themselves of wood or trees from the forest, must ancestrally, seek permission before doing so, (Act4 Sc.2). Additionally, the strict rule of taking only what is needed, and nothing more, informs a conservationist and environmentally conscious attitude towards nature among the African slaves, in general. This is seen in the Maroon Scene in Act 5 Sc. 2, where it highlights slave Elders perpetuating the Papa Bois folktale, by demonstrating this practice of paying homage to the *Guardian of the Forest*, before trees can be cut down; in order to build Gang-Gang Sarah's slave cabin.

The scene also highlights another transplantation of African cultural practices in the region, seen in their style of singing as a group, where one person/leader sings and others/group respond. This is presented several times in the play, to reinforce the oral nature of the environment, which necessitates imparting knowledge through word of mouth, instead of writing down.

- ❖ **The Silk Cotton Tree**

The silk cotton tree is said to have a soul or resident spirit, as well as dead souls living in its roots and branches. In fact, silk cotton trees are rumoured, in the Caribbean region, to move about and gather, to consult with one another. Furthermore, men dealing in witchcraft or [15]***Obeahmen***, as they are popularly called in the Caribbean region, are said to cast spells on people, by driving a nail into the silk cotton tree, as they call on evil spirits to cause someone's soul to leave his/her body and live in the tree. The silk cotton tree was also believed to be sacred by African slaves transported to the Caribbean during the Plantation era, because they believed their ancestors lived in its branches and that the great snake god, Damballah, also lived inside it. This tree, scientifically known as *Bombax ceiba*, grows to over 200 feet tall, and lives over hundreds of years; is one of the largest trees on the island of Tobago and well-known for the Gang-Gang Sarah legend, which is linked to it.

In Act 4 Sc. 5, an *Obeahman* is consulted by clients for assistance in the African magical arts. Slaves on the Plantation are afraid for their lives, because Mr. Bristol, the Plantation Owner, has given them orders to clear some land with a silk cotton tree on it; to extend his cane-field. The feared, but revered silk cotton tree stands in the selected path, and slaves are very fearful of the consequences of cutting down this special tree, with its black magic links to evil spirits, ancestors, and those whose spirits have been nailed there. Therefore, there is pending doom for the Bristol family, if the tree is not saved; a consequence of which the Bristol twins' lives hang in the balance. Anancy also reinforces the importance of the silk cotton tree at the end of the scene and warns of the danger of interfering with it, (Act 4. Sc. 1). This confirms the legend of the tree and the cultural importance it holds for Gang-Gang Sarah at the end of the play.

Call-And-Response

The **Call-and-Response**[16], is a generic style of singing, also used in some types of storytelling, where there is a succession of two phrases; the first phrase is *called* and the second *responds* to it, especially between a speaker and an audience/listener. However, nowhere is the *Call-and-Response* genre more visible than in Act 4. The Biblical story that Ade, a Muslim African, hears from the English Plantation family is about a slave uprising – the story of Moses and Pharaoh, who refuses to let God's people go. Ade's fascination with the tale centres around the audacity of Moses, (a *slave*), who boldly challenges King Pharaoh (*a superior person*); is, at face value, quite awe-inspiring to him. Retelling this story to a group of slaves, as he *hears* it, he responds to the story, by focusing only on the part which has significance for them as slaves – i.e., a slave having the audacity to rebel against a master, (Act 4 Sc.4).

However, the rousing sentiment of defiance that the song evokes, as the slaves dance to it, creates two perspectives: Ade's, which is passively and uncritically just passing on what hears; so superficially it is a tale that he just '*passes on'*. However, the song he sings to the group, which is also called, **"Pass It On,"** takes on a different meaning among the slaves, (Act 4 Sc.4). Here, there is the birth of an oral skill that will, later in the play, (also seen in Anancy's interventions and interjections), become the chief means by which information, wisdom and knowledge is transmitted among the slaves. Therefore, given the oral nature of the environment, this practice highlights the emergence of an early Caribbean *'literature,'* with its origin in West African oral narratives and Amerindian roots. Later, other literary input, such as Asian and European components, added to the body of early Caribbean works, are traceable to proverbs, riddles, speechifying, children's song-games, and tales of African oral literature, respectively.

Additionally, the type of stick-dance that the men perform, the [17]*Kalinda* dance, (also known as *Calinda*, the French spelling, and *Calenda,* the Spanish equivalent); is a type of folk music and war dance, that was a transplanted slave practice into the Caribbean region from Africa in the I720's; mainly presented as a combat skill among the slaves. Therefore, in Act 4, this practice reflects the slaves' mood and motive behind the dance during Ade's **call,** to which his audience **responds.**

Christianization of Slaves

Ade's behaviour in Act 4 is important because later on, he misconstrues what he *sees*, which results in, unconsciously or inadvertently, influencing the slaves' choice to become Christians. Therefore, in Act 4 Sc. 3, seeing Christians being baptised in a stream, followed by renaming, (an act which resembles the slaves' marine spirit possession and ancestral worship in Africa), Ade is influenced to *'follow'* Christianity. Slaves, being already acquainted with water and marine spirits, were drawn to this type of religion, accepted baptism in running water, where they felt they would encounter and be possessed by marine spirits. This became a form of ancestral worship, that synthesized or converged with Christianity in the region, since many slaves accepting this form of Christianity, were misled to believe that it represented their own ancestral worship.

Notwithstanding this, Ade's Plantation owner, the Bristol family, refused to call him a *Christian*; choosing to identify him as a *"follower"* only, since he was not white. Simultaneously, Ade is *following* what he witnesses, and he in turn, *teaches/passes it on* to others. The wider significance of *'passing on'* tradition, permeated slave culture in the Plantation's oral environment, since it was a strategy of ensuring and maintaining group understanding and solidarity. For example, Act 3: Scenes 4 and 5, where the slaves conducted a ritual deep in the woods, present a very illuminating picture of the extent slaves would go, to ensure practice and survival of their African culture; despite its prohibition and the threat of harsh repercussions from Slave owners.

Slave Owners' Prohibitions

- ❖ **Kumina Rituals**

An example of a prohibition among the slaves was the [18]*Kumina* ritual practice, a form of religious dance. In some areas of the Caribbean, the *Kumina* ritual (also referred to as *Shango* in Grenada and Trinidad), was forbidden on Plantations, for fear that it might encourage rebellion and instil defiance against Plantation Owners' rules. Today, *Kumina* is described as one of the most African religious expression surviving in Jamaica today. The language and the dances of *Kumina* are still untainted, and can be traced to tribes in the Congo in Africa. In Jamaica, the rituals are usually associated with wakes, burials, or memorial services, but can also be performed in a range of other cultural experiences. For example, *Kumina* rituals are used when help is needed to gain certain types of advantages, such as winning a court case or conquering an adversary. Equally, its entertainment value has been displayed in dance performances by the National Dance Theatre of Jamaica and other groups around the world. However, many people associate *Kumina* with suspicion, claiming it to be a form of witchcraft or obeah. In Act 3 Sc. 4, this ritual took place deep in the woods, overseen by *"Lookouts"* to warn the slaves of Plantation Managers' detection of their prohibited activity. Understandably, the original ritual is performed in a trance-like state, associated with drinking animals' blood for power, with some of the participants falling down under spiritual influence, during the ceremonies. *Kumina* and *Shango* are characterized by ritual dance, spiritual healing, spirit possession, sacrificial offerings, spiritual powers, as well as the celebration of ancestor powers. It is for these reasons they are feared in certain circles, but those who know more about this religious expression have advised against labelling *Kumina* as superstition, and equally, warned against its use for bad purposes.

Notwithstanding the prohibition against such cultural practice on sugar Plantations, the passing on of information and knowledge among slaves took other forms. For example, Gang-Gang Sarah established her altars, and moved among the people, secretly giving advice, help, guidance, knowledge of African spiritual and cultural practices, at times in open defiance of Plantation rules. She helped those in childbirth and used her African cultural knowledge to help the slaves to rebel against rules; commit infanticide, taught the art of poisoning, combat, and how to use their bodies through dancing, to heal themselves, (Act 3 Sc. 4). Moreover, her skill in using bush medicine to great advantage, are all reflective of the practices of African herbalists and witch doctors in Africa today.

❖ **Marriage**

The ideal of marriage, as a lifelong bond between a couple, was not an option on Plantations because slaves were regarded as chattel property. Given this situation, Slave-owners made all decisions, and this was born out in Act 5 Sc. 1, when Mr. Bristol, the Plantation owner, decided to speedily force slave men and women to form involuntary unions on his plantation. This was based on a financial outcome, for two reasons:

(1). It was a strategy to increase his slave numbers on his Plantation in the region by relying on home-grown slave capital; slaves being born in the island, instead of costly raids from Africa.

(2). It was also to prevent the risks of his 'human cargo' being reduced on Slave ships, through disease, death, or shrinkage of 'stock' due to slaves throwing themselves overboard, during the Transatlantic crossing.

Furthermore, marriage among slaves remained a prohibition with slave-owners, who also used conniving ways to break ties in relationships among their slaves. Consequently, if couples who secretly chose mates were caught, having [19]**"jumped the broomstick;"** (their own traditional form of marriage), owners would violate the enslaved couples' marriages, by forcing the women to serve them as their own concubines; which frequently resulted in having mixed race children with the slaves. Another motive behind this form of repeated oppression, was the fact that mixed race children fetched a high price in slave auctions.

In contrast, marriage among non-slaves was considered both a civil and religious Right since they had legal standing. However, it meant that for the slaves, seen as 'property,' with no standing or recognisable Rights in society, it was impossible for them to enter contracts of any kind. Intimate bonds among slaves continuously sustained brokenness in slavery. This therefore highlights the significance in Act 5, of Gang-Gang Sarah and Tom's marriage, as an act of defiance, as well as triumph, over yet another form of oppression. Their story therefore dramatizes the dilemma of enslaved people, who chose to pursue their true love and risk the heart-wrenching consequences. A symbolism of that defiance is seen in Act 5 Sc 7, when Joe and Nennen, (the oldest slaves on the Plantation), officiated the *'jumping over the broomstick.'* Traditionally, they were sanctioning Tom and Gang-Gang Sarah's marriage against the odds. Effectively, such defiance also symbolises a resurrection of a prohibited traditional practice that was now being firmly transplanted in the new environment, as a cultural and traditional Right.

Matriarchal Dominance

In Act 3 Sc. 5, Gang-Gang Sarah, having witnessed a slave in the middle of childbirth, who was still being beaten and forced to work, is instrumental, in saving the baby from its dying mother, with the assistance of the elderly slave women's cultural and traditional know-how. The Matriarchs, who always seek spiritual confirmation before acting, passed on their traditional customs to the younger women as is seen in the healing dance. Due to their prohibited status, these and many other rituals were conducted deep in the woods, in secret bush-meetings thus enabling the undiluted survival of some of these practices on Caribbean Plantations.
As a matriarch, Gang-Gang Sarah, displays an indomitable warrior spirit throughout the play, as she grows to understand her role in

slave society, as *"one who would lead."* At the beginning of the play, she stands out as one whose strength of character sets her apart and consequently this presents problems to those who want to constrain her, (Act 3 Sc. 2). She escapes from the *Hunters of the Shadows* who had to doubly restrain her. In (Act 2 Sc. 1), she stands defiantly in the storm on board the Slave ship and petitions the African Orishas, with promises of continued worship to them, in exchange for their safe crossing on the Atlantic Ocean to the Caribbean, (Act 2 Sc. 2). Having newly arrived in the Caribbean environment, she prematurely challenges a Slave Handler, for which she receives a near-death punishment; until her life's mission is revealed to the elderly matriarchs, who nursed her back to consciousness, (Act 3 Sc. 3).

She is a Birth Attendant or [20]***Doula***; one with spiritual prowess and cultural knowledge of the arts of African spirituality to heal, including the Bristol family's children, (Act 4 Sc. 6). She is the lead member among the slaves, to share their monthly ration of corn and is promoted to being Plantation Birth Attendant by the Slave Owner himself, due to her leadership qualities, (Act 5 Sc. 1). We witness her growing importance among the slaves, who respect and acknowledge her specialism.

Gang-Gang Sarah's importance in bridging the gap between the 'old' and 'new' world environments is therefore shown in her retention, teaching and practice of African spirituality and knowledge of the culture, which she passes on. She also uses such knowledge to protect others, to direct and co-ordinate roles and behaviour among the slaves; before, during and after the rebellion, at the end of the play, (Act 5 Sc. 6). Her portrayal is one that highlights the image of a *"strong black woman;"* as is sometimes depicted in texts, 'mothering' and also 'fathering' her children. Grass-roots activists and Reparationists, have linked this phenomenon to the psychology of disempowered male slaves, whose forced involuntary unions during slavery became, and in some cases still is, the *modus operandi* reverberating in relationships among black couples today. The image of the strong black woman, (often projected as aggressive and warrior-like), is still prevalent among 21st century Caribbean women, who are often bringing up children on their own, whilst battling against Eurocentric conventions of female behaviour, that project them as being at odds with their ideals of femininity.

African Deities, Christianity & Indigenous Religions

The **Glossary** of this play presents a detailed description of the various African deities or Orishas referred to in this play, as those which were brought into the region during the early days of slavery. These Orishas would have been predominantly worshipped among the slaves, since they were the greatest in numbers in the region's population. Today, this is dominated in the region by Christianity, Hinduism, and Islam. However, the African-derived religions are just as resilient in the region's mixed environment, since African Orisha worship and Trinidadian/Tobagonian indigenous tribal (Caribs and Arawak's) religions are still practiced among some people. This still consists of a range of African religious beliefs and rituals, as practised during the periods of slavery in the Caribbean.

The play suggests such worship-forms have been influenced by Christian traditions; seen in Ade and Edith's conversion to Christianity in Act 4; exemplified in their linking this to African marine worship. Also, these two characters' divided loyalties, projected in Act 5 Scenes 4 and 5, highlight Ade and Edith's ambivalence about which side they should take in the imminent rebellion and destruction of the Bristol family's Plantation. Ade and Edith's emotional state stems firstly, from their feelings of inferiority. Secondly, their inability to discredit their master's severe abusive treatment, stems from confusion, engendered by their mixed religious and other day-to-day experiences. Ade believes what he hears – that the *"Talking Book"* (the Bible), has given their master authority to abuse them with impunity, as something they should accept and 'obey'. Yet his overriding problem is his inability to interpret such forms of oppression as the Bristol's terrorism of their human spirit and projected supremacy;

so, he willingly accepts Christianity. Consequently, the Christian religion forced them to become grateful for their subjugated lifestyles, (Act 4 Sc. 3).

Additionally, in following Christianity, Slaves were made to reject all African forms of worship and culture, believing, as they were told, that they were, *'washed white from the inside,'* (Act 5 Sc 4), based on Ade and Edith's conversion. In other words, the play suggests Christian/African fusions, maintained an emphasis on Christianity, to enforce psychological subordination. Added to such forms of brainwashing, was the converted slaves' belief that some forms of Christian worship were synonymous with worshipping marine spirits, as was practised in Africa. Later, they recognised the Plantation Owner's double standards when, in desperation, he accepted the *'black'* medicine, when the *'white'* medicine given by a qualified British doctor, had no efficacy, to save their dying children.

The play presents Ade as a silent protagonist; a position that enables him to *'pass on'* what he witnesses. In contrast, the Bristol family's boastful discussions at the dinner table with guests, about their lucrative slave trading business, (Act 4 Sc. 1), whilst simultaneously lauding the Bible, show how their brand of inhumanity is clearly at odds with their professed Christian values. The Slave Owners make it clear, using Biblical reference, their justification for keeping slaves, though their practices are far from Christian, as they adopt the moral high ground, (Act 4 Sc. 1). However, given the recorded contesting role of Christianity in the environment, there were rebel slave leaders who were staunch Christians, but also fiercely anti-colonial. An example is Paul Bogle in the 1865 uprising in Jamaica. Bogle was a Baptist, a sect which generally opposed the colonial order, which became synonymous with the Anglican church, was more pronounced after Emancipation.

Religion is also presented in Act 4 Sc. 7, with a debate involving the three African gods, in a contest of wills, about the role that the individual should adopt, in determining justice. The presentation of this religious pantheon, projects gods with human-like qualities. It presents [21]**Gamab**, as the African God of life, death, and renewal; a kindly god, in contest against [22]**Gaunab**, his arch enemy and god of evil. The gods are personified individually: one who is reputed to be peaceful and forgiving, represents a leader's non-violent approach to life. The other, who is warlike, violent, and trades tit-for-tat, is unlike the first; represents the rebellious leader. Finally, [23]**Eshu** who is also called Papa Legba, turns up as a messenger, on behalf of the [24]**Supreme God Olodumare**; with a message to Gang-Gang Sarah, to maintain stability on the plantation, by helping to preserve life. This scene, in Act 4 Sc. 7, presents the African religions as "spiritual powers," which the slaves tenaciously adhered to, as coping strategies; given the severity of life on Sugar plantations.

However, this play highlights the importance of the African religions in the Caribbean environment, as it relates to Gang-Gang Sarah, it must be said that such a focus, is not meant to overlook the existence of the original inhabitants of the region or their own religious practices. In the pre-Columbian and colonial eras, two tribal groups, (the Caribs and Arawaks), were the indigenous people of the Caribbean. This population had their own Amerindian religious pantheon, existing alongside fused colonial Christianity, as well as African religious practices. Like Christianity, both the Arawaks and Caribs possessed a notion of a high god, but this differed from the Christian God. Aboriginal high gods were thought to exert little direct influence on the workings of the universe. In fact, they believed that the Arawakan god was not self-created but was given birth by a mother with five identities and names. Most deities in the Arawak pantheon were also recognised by several different appellations. They believed that there existed an earth mother and a sky father, like that of American Indian groups. One of the most important differences between Arawak and Carib religions is that Arawaks worshiped nature, as well as their ancestors; believing that the bones of their dead leaders had power in them. On the other hand, the Caribs believed in several spirit beings, as well as a high god; the highest in their pantheon was the moon, (then the sun) because they measured time according to lunar cycles. Much later, the different colonisers (British, French, Dutch, Spanish), brought their own brand of religions, to the region, which created a culturally and religiously fused environment.

Importance of the Dances in the Play

The play's final Act, with the slaves' feeling triumphant after their successful rebellion, presents a microcosm of the wider context of the abolition of slavery in 1836, a period of the greatest watershed event in the history of the Caribbean. The liberation of the slaves, led by Jabari (Act 5 Sc 5), re-enacts the emancipation of slaves from the trauma of imprisonment of their bodies, minds, and spirits. Given the Play's timeline, from the slaves' entry into the Caribbean region, to rebellion and freedom, it can be said to symbolically reflect the hundreds of years of bondage against the backdrop of their various counter-resistance. Therefore, the essence of the celebratory dancing is also a form of catharsis for the slaves; a symbolic purging of their minds, bodies, spirits from the bondage, fear, hurt and harm they endured, (Act 5 Sc. 7). Evidently, the sentiments expressed in the vibrancy of the music and dances, reflect the celebratory nature of Emancipation Day, 1st August 1836, and showcase such achievement as a form of moral and spiritual triumph or renewal.

The mixed dances provide evidence of reasons why Caribbean music has a unique blend of features: from the colonizing influence of European countries, the indigenous tribes, to those of the 46 million Africans brought into the region. The dances throughout this play show how a synthesis of dance cultures may have taken place over the years; shown in the characters' showcase of the various inputs in the play's Finale, in Act 5 Sc. 7. The contesting styles show how rhythm and body movements highlight the rhythm and beat of the drums; represent the African input. These have been included to show that improvisation has taken place. For example, where the spoon, scraper, and the [25]**tamboo-bamboo** instruments are used, they became new percussive instruments in the Caribbean environment that replaced the prohibited African *"Talking"* drums.

The characters' awareness of the style of the European influences, as seen in the [26]***Quadrille* dance**, is clearly different in harmony, melody, and pace, and we see their choice of the vibrancy of the African musical features, over the *Quadrille* in Act 5 Sc. 7. However, what is important in the music and dance in the final Act (Act 5) of this play, is the evidence of a fusion, which suggests that Caribbean musical forms are best understood by their various inputs into the region, since the styles of dances and musical origin, contextualise their historic inclusion and informs us of how they were used. For example, whether in social events (*Gang-Gang's wedding*), religious events as ceremonial (*Kumina*), or recreational *(Kalinda)* activities, they evidence historic influences in their creative retentions.

Work Songs used in the Play

Similarly, the included songs give us insight into the thoughts and feelings of the slaves; whether in expressing their lament or the Kalinda display with the '*Pass it on'* song; inspired courage and bravery in the face of the slaves' debilitating hardship, (Act 4 Sc. 4). During slavery, Work Songs were used firstly to remind the Africans of home. Some were sung to raise morale as they worked, with the help of collective rhythm. In other words, they functioned as a means of maintaining sanity, instilling hope, garnering strength, and group support for one another.

❖ **The Corn Work-Song**

The Corn Work-song, sung in Act 4 Sc. 2, is included to give an example of how food became the subject of work-songs on plantations. Corn, which was grown by the slaves for their upkeep, became their staple diet; naturally, it found its way in songs, since it dominated their lives. Today, in the Caribbean, corn is still part of some meals; in dishes such as [27]***Corn meal porridge, Coo-coo, cankey,*** etc. It is also sung about in children's song-games e.g. "*My*

Ship Sails, how many men on deck?" when children play a guessing number-game with individual corn kernels.

❖ The Sugar-Cane Work-Song

Songs about cane also found their way into the slaves' repertoire, sung by adult slaves because during planting, tending, and harvesting, the songs accompanied the slaves' work, (Act 4 Sc. 2). This aspect of the slaves' lives can be interpreted as a bitter-sweet experience, because cane is literally *sweet* to taste but, it is also born out of a *bitter* experience.

Overall, songs have been used in this play to function as a means of overcoming hardship and simultaneously, to express anger and frustration, by taking the form of both creativity and opposition; hidden in the songs. As mentioned above, the most common feature of the early Caribbean songs was the call-and-response style, as seen in Act 4 Sc. 4. This characteristic feature of the work-song later found its way in spiritual songs; especially when slaves were converted to Christianity. It is also a style that can be seen in Gospel music and the Blues, today.

Other Notable Vocal Influencers

Slaves also used cunning ways to communicate with one another and this is evident in some creative noises that were used to exclude the Plantation Master. It is a practice that created specific sounds for warning, calling a gathering, (in the absence of the *'Talking'* drum) and used percussive instruments, (e.g., bottles and other sharp instruments) to communicate. Evidence of this is seen in Act 1 Sc 2, when Jabari, Seth and Abi were able to interpret a nearby sound as signalling danger to which he took action to kill the unidentified person who was hiding in the bush, when he attempted to use his voice to instigate trouble for them. Also, in Act 3 Sc. 4, when *"Lookouts"* interrupted a religious ritual in the bush, with vocal signals that abruptly ended their secret religious ritual. Plantation masters used to fear slave uprising, so they initiated prohibition of drums, which they realised were used by the slaves to *'talk'* among themselves. However, despite its ban, the practice went underground; hence, the slaves' creation of new percussive sounds in the Caribbean. It is for this reason, towards the end of the play, Gang-Gang Sarah's instruction to the slaves, when co-ordinating the rebellion, is for them to bring out their *"hidden drums,"* to communicate in the traditional way, not only among themselves but directly to their African deities.

Slave Merchants and the Slave Trade

Finally, the overriding theme of the play is Slavery: The Slave Trade, as well as the role of Slave Merchants, Slave Masters, and enablers of the Slave Trade. Far from being only fiction, the play reflects a Caribbean history of the Slave Trade, made possible by colonisation and empire building; that not only built Britain, but as intimated by Peter Bristol in Act 4 Sc 1, may have also fuelled the Industrial Revolution. The play's Bristol family takes their name from Bristol, in England; a city in the north of England; which became, by 1730, Britain's main slaving port.

Merchants from Bristol traded freely with Europe, the Barbary Coast of North Africa, America, and the Caribbean. By the mid-1660s tobacco, sugar and other raw materials in the Caribbean and America were imported in large quantities. They were grown on colonised/European-owned plantations in the Caribbean, by slaves who were kidnapped, bought, and sold from Africa and transported to work there. (Act 4 Sc. 1) During this time, the London-based Royal African Company had control over all trade with Africa. They excluded all other British ports, in their trade of ivory, gold, dyewood, and spices, which was used to buy slaves from Africans who assisted them with capture. One notable name during this period is Edward Colston (1636-1721), the son of a Bristol merchant who was involved in the Transatlantic slave trade as a member of the Royal African Company. Colston traded in cloth and wine from Europe, and sugar from the Caribbean. But by 1698, Bristol merchants became totally involved in the African Slave Trade, because the Royal Africa Company no longer had the monopoly to trade with Africa.

The situational irony here is, far from being only one group or family of slave traders, there were many people in Bristol who benefitted from the Slave Trade. For example, the sea captains who filled their ship with slaves to transport across the Atlantic Ocean were paid for their work, (Act 4). There were also businessmen, who funded slave ship voyages, taking the profits for themselves. Additionally, small businesses and craftsmen who supplied the trade goods that were exchanged for enslaved Africans, (Act 4) were also paid for their part in the trading chain. Manual labour was also provided by dockworkers, who unloaded the cargoes of sugar, rum and cotton from the plantations in the Americas; they, were paid for their day's work. Furthermore, there was a vast amount of people throughout Britain, who benefitted, both directly and indirectly, from the trade in 'human cargo.' The wealth gained through this trade also funded new ships, buildings, charitable works and industrial projects in Britain. Such was this lucrative trade that when Colston died, he left today's equivalent of £5million pounds, to various Bristol charities and churches. Bristol town, by 1750, had transported some 8,000 of the 20, 000 enslaved Africans, who were sent that year to the British Caribbean and North America, before the trade was surpassed by Liverpool that year.

In Act 4 Sc. 1, the Bristol family project their bombastic perspectives on their burgeoning slave trade in the Caribbean, in discussions around their dinner table, that show how prevalent their brand of inhumanity was at odds with the Christian values they purport to uphold. The men make it clear, with reference from the Bible, that their slave trade is sanctioned by God, to justify their sinister acts. In fact, their excesses at the dinner-table in Act 4 Sc. 1, present dramatic irony; counter-balanced in Scene 2, where the slaves' grim reality, is a celebration of their anticipated measly bag of cornmeal each month.

Another theme in the play is rebellion against slavery and those who perpetrate it. This is seen in Act 5 Sc. 5, when Jabari, the self-styled leader and Revolutionary amongst the slaves, instigated uprisings, and rebellions against Plantation Owners. His style of rebellion resembles actions taken by Toussaint Louverture, the first successful slave revolt leader from the Republic of Haiti, in 1791. Louverture had led a successful rebellion and emancipated the slaves in the French colony of Saint-Domingue (Haiti). In this play, in Act 5 Sc. 6, rumours of plantations being burned down, led by the Jabari, with Louverturean spirit and Anancy-like cunning, evade detection and triumph over the Plantation owners. Jabari had instructed slaves to deceive their masters, feign ignorance of instructions, work *very* slowly, break tools, and other acts of insubordination; (Act 5 Sc. 5). During slavery, rebellion included ridiculing masters and overseers with humorous tales, witty jokes, and satirical songs, as resistive acts, whilst using Anancy stories, to outwit them. However, the stories within this play, with their historical contexts, are not only fixed in the past; their thematic concerns are constantly being re-visited and re-evaluated, with succeeding generations as they become acquainted and re-acquainted with the content and the context of past experiences.

    The Introduction of this Play stated that it was a work of fiction, based on the story of Gang-Gang Sarah, a Caribbean folk legend. As with all lore, legends, early literature and/or their histories, these orally transmitted beliefs from one generation to another, show that despite the passage of time, this tale has been indelibly etched in the subconscious of the Caribbean people. Being transferred symbolically, as a cultural heirloom, such tales evidence a fusion of Africa's deep consciousness within the people's psyche, through their recreated lore and evaluation of the past, as they try to make sense of the presence.

    A case in point is the present political situation globally, five centuries later, with re-examination of historical acts and their consequences from a 21st century perspective. This year (2020) has seen displays of global unrests, by people protesting vehemently against institutional and other forms of racism. The world-wide scenes of solidarity sparked by police brutality in the USA, of black people some believe, is a repercussion of histories that are directly linked to past atrocities, such as slavery. The resultant global outpouring of mass unity in a movement struggling for truth, humanity, and justice, has ignited/re-ignited debates on slavery, and the part played by those who have been previously idolised, as a result of this trade.

It would seem that as the value of historical figures are re-examined, so are cultural heroes, heroines, and legendary figures, with reassessment of the values they currently hold in our society. As far as [27]**Edward Colston** is concerned, many in Britain no longer glorify him as a slave-trading hero of the 1600's. Instead, the 'tide' has turned against him, in preference for a rejection and desecration of his name and effigy, in the 21st century. Edward Colston's egregious involvement in the Slave trade has been re-evaluated in 2020, so that a bronze memorial to the 17th-century slave merchant, was pulled down during a [29]**Black Lives Matter** protest in the UK, on 7th June 2020. The statute, which had been erected in the city centre since 1895, was toppled and later dumped in Bristol harbour. Then, it was thrown in the water near Pero's Bridge - named in honour of an enslaved man.

Therefore, with the currency of re-assessing the values of cultural assets generally, it is hoped that reassessment will also ignite debates on the importance of Gang-Gang Sarah's life story; so that she will be given the national historical and cultural prominence she deserves. Resurrecting Gang-Gang Sarah from her apparent skeletal framework and infusing it with vibrant content that breathes life into her importance in the Caribbean, gives her fresh living impetus, so that she can take her rightful place along other cultural antecedents; is the main aim of this writer.

Reading the Play

Since all plays are written to be performed, or dramatically read out aloud, it is hoped that in dramatizing the characters' action through their speaking, and the audience listening to them as they tell their own stories, will contribute to the overall structure and enjoyment of the play. We follow the chronology of the events that led to Gang-Gang's arrival and role-modelling in the Caribbean, as well as the cumulative dramatic effect that this sensational character's life impacts on characters in the play. These will range from opinions, the physicality of the performance on stage and the variety of reactions from audiences. The play is divided into five acts, with scenes identified by their thematic concerns, as they progress with individual characters, until the *Finale.* These acts enable easily identifiable sections of the play for detailed study, which can be achieved in reading, experimenting, and rehearsing in small groups. The variety of themes can be meaningfully explored to discover depth and understanding of the characters presented in the play.

Roselle Thompson
London 2020

NOTES TO THE INTRODUCTION

1. **Agoji warriors** - the Agoji warrior women (the name originating from French) were commonly referred to as the **Dahomey Amazons**, from the kingdom of Dahomey. *(See Glossary 33).*
2. **Mise-en-abime** occurs within a text when there is a duplication or reduplication of images and concepts that refer to the text. For example, the Play, *Gang-Gang Sarah*, is based on the character Gang-Gang Sarah as the main narrative or frame story. This main narrative is designed to set the stage and lead the reader/audience from this first story, into multiple narratives or, in this case, sub-plays, that illuminate thematic concerns within the play.
3. **National Library & Information Systems Authority,(NAILS)** Government of Trinidad and Tobago;www.nails.gov.tt
4. **Igbo/Ibo** are people living chiefly in south eastern Nigeria who speak Igbo, a language of the Benue-Congo branch of the Niger-Congo language family.
5. **Congo** - The Congo or **Kongo** people are a Bantu ethnic group primarily defined as the speakers of Kikongo (Kongo languages). They lived along the Atlantic coast of Central Africa, in a region that by the 15th century was a centralized and well-organized Kingdom of Kongo but is now a part of three countries.
6. **Ibibio** - The Ibibio people are a coastal people in southern Nigeria. They are mostly found in Akwa Ibom, Cross River, and on the Eastern Part of Abia. The Ibibio people are Kwa speaking people Benue-Congo group of Niger-Congo language.
7. **Malinke** or the **Mandinka** are a West African ethnic group, primarily found in southern Mali, eastern Guinea, and northern Ivory Coast. They speak slight variations of the broad Mande branch of the Niger-Congo family of languages.

8. **Cédula of Population:** see also, Eric Williams, *History of the people of Trinidad and Tobago*, (London 1964).
9. **Creole identity**, a person of mixed European and black decent, e.g. Spanish and French.
10. **J. J. Thomas*, The Theory and Practice of Creole Grammar*** (1969;1869), New Beacon Books, London & Port-of-Spain, Trinidad.
11. **Caribs, Arawaks & Tainos** – the first peoples of the Caribbean and of the twin-island republic – Trinidad and Tobago. They were Amerindians tribes, from as early as 8000BC, until the present. (See *Introduction* for more details).
12. **Anancy, Brer Anancy, Anansi, Ananse or Mrs. Anancy** - is a direct transfer tale from West Africa to the Caribbean. It is the most popular of all the African folktales that were taken to the Caribbean via the slaves. *(See Glossary 19)*
13. **Crick-crack** *stories* – This African folk tale tradition is well known and practised within the Caribbean territories. Whilst some may vary in renditions, they are all variants from a common origin. One major characteristic in the storytelling is that it **embodies performance.** *(See Glossary 36)*
14. **Papa Bois** – Papa Bois lives in the forest and he is the *'father or protector'* of the forest and animals that live there. He is known by many names including "**Maître Bois**" (master of the woods) and "**Daddy Bouchon**" (hairy man). *(See Glossary 18)*
15. **Call-and-response** – (in *music* and some forms of *storytelling*): a style where there's a succession of two phrases; the first phrase is heard and the second responds to it, especially between speaker and audience/listener *(See Glossary 16)*
16. **Obeah man** – A person who practices sorcery or witchcraft, known as **voodoo** in the Caribbean. Such persons were known for casting spells or unleashing spiritual powers against their targeted victims or enemies.

17. **Kalinda,** with various spellings - *Calenda / Caleinda / Calinda / Corlinda / Kalenda / Kallinder*. In Trinidad Kalinda began as a combative stick-fighting ritual which was later transformed into a dance to the drum and shack-shack in the plantations during colonial times. *(See Glossary 34)*
18. **Kumina** is one of the most African religious expression in the Caribbean, (especially Jamaica), with its roots originating from the Congo region of Central Africa. The ritual is characterized by ritual dance, spiritual healing, spirit possession, sacrificial offerings, spiritual powers, as well as the celebration of ancestor powers.
(See Glossary 20)
19. **Jumping the broomstick** – The practice of *"jumping the broomstick"* originates from Ghana, West Africa. The broom in Asante and other Akan cultures also held spiritual value and symbolized sweeping away past wrongs or removing evil spirits. Brooms were waved over the heads of marrying couples to ward off spirits.
(See Glossary 35)
20. **Doula** or **Birth Attendant** is someone who assists a woman in labour to deliver her baby. The word *"doula"* derives from **Greek**, meaning a *'helper'* or *'caregiver.'*
(See Glossary 30)
21. **Gamab** - Supreme God of life, death and seasonal renewal. **Gamab** lives in the sky and directs the fate of mankind. *(See Glossary 25)*
22. **Gaunab** – **Gaunab**, the god of evil and death. He is an enemy of Gamab, and Tsui-Goab. He created the Rainbow.
(See Glossary 27)
23. **Eshu** – the name Eshu varies around the world in rituals honouring these deities. Eshu, also called **Exu** (pronounced "Eshoo"), is not an Orisha, or Lwa, but are earthly guardians of the luminal, who are both a force of nature, as well as spirits of the dead. *(See Glossary 12)*
24. **Olodumare** – (**Yoruba:** *O-lo-dù-ma-rè*) also known as **Ọlọrun** (Almighty) is the name given to one of the three

manifestations of the Supreme God or Supreme Being. *(See Glossary 3)*
25. **Tamboo-bamboo instruments** – an ensemble made up of different lengths and sizes of bamboo which, when pounded to the ground, simulated musical sounds of music; soprano, alto, tenor and bass. *(See Glossary 38)*
26. **Quadrille** –A quadrille is a type of dance for four couples, with each couple forming a single side of a square. *(See Glossary 37)*
27. **Corn meal porridge, Coo-coo, cankey** – Caribbean foods made from cornmeal and water with added spices and milt to taste. Cornmeal has minerals and vitamins like thiamine, B6, folate, selenium, manganese, phosphorus, iron, and magnesium. Unlike flour cornmeal is corn grains and not contain gluten. It is given to Caribbean babies to wean them off breast milk.
28. **Edward Colston** - was an English merchant, who was involved in the Atlantic Slave Trade in the 17th century. Colston was a British Conservtive Member of Parliament, who made his fortune through human suffering. Between 1672 and 1689, ships are believed to have transported about 80,000 men, women, and children from Africa to the Caribbean and Americas.
29. **"Black Lives Matter" protest** – A Movement *"operating as non-political, non-partisan, non-violence Black Lives Matter platform, operating in a humanitarian capacity and concern before all else. They represent those of all ethnicities and from all nations who believe in racial equality, are anti-racists, we stand together, we can choose to kneel together in peace and solidarity asserting black people are treated as equals to white people and is a human right to receive racial equality, social and criminal justice in the societies we live together, as full citizens of the country and as a united nation."*
www.blacklivesmatter.uk

Gang-Gang Sarah:

A Caribbean Sensation

CHARACTERS

Anancy
Gang-Gang Sarah
Tom - *Gang-Gang Sarah's slave husband*
Peter Bristol – *Slave Merchant & Plantation Owner*
Mrs Bristol (wife)
Stella Bristol – *son (twin)*
Peter Bristol - *daughter (twin)*
The Bristol's *Dinner Guests*
Dr. Evans – *a medical doctor*
Edith - *House slave*
Ade – *House slave*
Jabari – *Rebel slave*
Abi – *Slave raider*
Seth – *Slave raider*
Mr. Murphy – *Slave trader*
Mr. Jeffrey – *Slave trader*
Babawalo – *Priest*
African Father
African Mother
Naming Ceremony Guests
African children
African Elders
Slave Handlers
Slave Manager
Stanjosef – *Obeah man*
Ana - *child slave*
Mary – *pregnant slave*
Nenen – *slave marriage official*
Old Joe - *slave marriage official*
Various Slaves *(male & female)*
Various spirits *(Gamab, Gaunab, Olodumare, Legba, Eshu)*

Locations: **Africa:Slave Ship:Caribbean Plantation**

ACT 1 SCENE 1 - WELCOME TO THE CARIBBEAN!

STAGE DIRECTION: *The stage is filled with lighting in soft Caribbean colours; red, gold, green, blue. The song of steel-pan music playing in the background, which fades.*

PROLOGUE

The Caribbean Song

Let me tell you a story, in this little Caribbean song,
Of our Caribbean islands, a peaceful region for long,
Which once was a haven for captured African slaves
Who brought Akan God of knowledge that was reshaped
Into Anancy, a trickster spider; queen of our storytelling
Made mischief on master,secretly passed culture in codes.
Oh Anancy, keeper of our stories, wit and wisdom so true,
Heart an' soul of Caribbean traditions, listen to her words.
Oh, Yes, it's Mrs. Anancy, just listen to her words!
Oh, Yes, it's Mrs Anancy, just listen to her words!

She will tell you our story, forged under the painful whip
Slavery, plantation, rebellion, then how our freedom came;
Sweet lands of our people, with blue seas and sunshine,
Laughing pretty women, leading jus' like men, big an' fine.
See their happy faces, when they jump in carnival an' whine,
But it wasn't always that easy; not an easy journey at all;
Now we eat ackee 'n saltfish, rice and peas, an' coo-coo,
Flying fish, oil down, curry goat, roti and lovely boiled food,
Drink strong rum, coconut water, enjoy life as we should;
Our culture is like a big flower-garden surround by the sea.
Sweet, sweet Caribbean islands –a place where we free!
Oh sweet beautiful islands, surrounded by lovely seas.

We born from a very long bitter-sweet plantation story,
Come with me, as I invite you to jus' sit, hear and see,
How an African woman became a Caribbean sensation;
A great legend in our midst:Gang-Gang Sarah is her name.
From Africa strong, solid as a rock, got whipped, Crack!

Skip! Jump to our Caribbean island; her new promised land.
Oh man, jus' listen to her story; you must listen very well,
How she fight for Caribbean people, so we can be free;
Man, jus' listen about Mama Caribbean, listen very well,
How she infuse us with African culture, her story I will tell.

You' better listen to Gang-Gang's story, listen very well!
'Bout Caribbean lands of many cultures, where we're free!
Oh sweet beautiful islands, surrounded by lovely seas.
Melting-pot of lovely people; mixed cultures, an' we're free!

STAGE DIRECTION: *A full steel-pan band plays and Anancy enters the stage, gliding in a spider-like manner. She has a sick in her hand which she stamps loudly once, at the beginning of her entrance. She then crawls all the way across to the other end of the stage; stops and stamps the stick loudly again - symbolising she is now taking charge of the proceedings. After prancing up and down to the music, she laughs out loudly, then prepares to address the audience directly. Moving closer to the edge of the stage, she points her stick towards the audience, each time she addresses them:*

ANANCY *(Enters in a jovial mood, laughing).* How-de-doo! How-de-doo! Welcome! E Kaaro o! Wha' happenin' deh? Que passa? *(Anancy laughs loudly)* Listen noh, I can speak French Creole too, you know, "Bonjou or bonswa!" Maybe some of you prefer, How you guys doing? Or What's up?
(Anancy laughs out loudly)
All-you hear about **Ananse?** The trickster spider who can speak all the languages and dialects of the world?
(Not waiting for an answer she prances to the background sound of steel band music, laughing).

ANANCY Yes, man! After all these long-long years, I can speak in everything, eh - English, French, Spanish, Dutch, German, Chinese, Japanese, Twi, Ga, Fanti, Yoruba, Patois, Creole, Nation Language, Street talk. You name it, you speak it speak it too. Yeah man! Standard or non-standard Anancy does it all! Is I Anancy mek it so! *(Laughs out loudly, as she continues dancing up and down).*

ANANCY *(Pointing to the audience)* So, whe' you come from? Maybe you hear 'bout **Bre Anancy** then? *(slight pause again, doesn't wait for an answer but prances to the sound of steel band music)* Dat is still me! *(She continues dancing to the music).*

ANANCY OK, OK! Hold-on nuh! *(Music pauses)* Then I know some of you hear about just plain ole '**Nancy stories,** yeah? *(Pauses again, doesn't wait for an answer but prances up and down to the sound of steel band music which gradually fades).* Listen man, it's still me; they're my stories!

ANANCY *(Laughing loudly)* So if that's the case, all-you know 'bout the **Crick-Crack** stories then? Eh heh? *(She laughs)* But that's about me too; Anancy in *all* the forms. *(She becomes serious temporarily).* Listen eh, ah go tell all-you a likely story! It's about how Africans became Caribbean people. *(Steelband music plays loudly as she prances left and right covering the length of the stage. She stops prancing but the music continues)*

ANANCY Listen, listen, <u>listen</u> noh!
(She stamps her stick defiantly, and the music stops immediately - she speaks to the audience in a half-whisper)

ANANCY I, Mrs. Anancy, go tell all-you a true, true '**Nancy** story! *(She laughs loudly).* Anancy knows it all! Yes, I Anancy, knows it all! Ha, Ha, hai!!
(She prances then stops, pauses, stamps her stick, points it at the crowd and calls out the traditional crick-crack to signal that storytime has begun).

ANANCY All-you ready to start? **CRICK!**
(The audience answers with gusto).

AUDIENCE CRACK!
(Addressing the audience, she speaks in Standard English, using her Broadcasting voice).

ANANCY Riddle me this, riddle me that! To destroy the sovereignty of a people, you must first destroy their **name:** this is directly linked to their history, their culture, their psychological well being; in fact, their total cultural Identity! But hear this noh! *(She whispers)* As it was in the beginning, so it will be in the end!

(Anancy shakes her head disapprovingly at what she has said, then she crawls off stage

[Exit Anancy

ACT 1 SCENE 2 - KIDNAP RAIDS ON VILLAGES

SETTING: A Camp somewhere in an African Forest
African Drumming: Jabari, a young rebel leader, with his accomplices, Seth and Abi, who is wounded, are gathered: the men, known as Hunters of the Shadows, have been conducting kidnap raids in local villages. (Jabari is armed with a bush-knife, spitting on the ground; He points his bush-knife at Seth, Abi's friend):

JABARI Abi, who the hell is this? Thought ah say no outsiders!
ABI He's Seth, the man I told you 'bout yesterday. He goin' to lead us to collect a group of boys near his village. Look, he can make our work light, plus he saved my life earlier today. Jus' look at my hand, I nearly bleed to death. And we could do with an extra pair of hands!
(Becoming furious, Jabari grabs Abi's collar and squares up to his face)
JABARI Need a hand? You're the one who'll lose a hand in a minute. Huh! I-d-i-ot! *(Angrily points his index finger at Abi's face).* YOU, making plans behind my back now?
ABI No-no-no boss! *(He cowers)*
JABARI No? Then how you know he's not a spy?
ABI But ah..........
JABARI *(Grabbing Abi again):* Listen, no damn butts....*I'm* leading this freakin' group, so *I* make the decisions – got it?
ABI Ok...Ok *(Abi backs away from the loosened grip. Seth interrupts, trying to diffuse the tense situation by kneeling down before Jabari in a servile manner)*
SETH I've a guarantee of over 50 men and women in a special place for you, Sah. As a childhood friend of Abi here, I give you my word, I can help you - please, Mr. Boss, sah.
ABI *(Pleading):* Look, Jabari, we're almost at the end of this thing. But we need a plan for the final raid tomorrow; there's talk about the raids and it's flying around, like women gossiping.
SETH Sah, we need to act real fast!
JABARI *(Contemplative)* Hush noh! I have a plan how we can

give those two white men, Murphy and Jeffrey, the amount of people they want; just in case they decide to take their business elsewhere.
(Grinnings mischievously) Listen, we'll do the last raid tomorrow. Then all that's left to do, is go and collect our money and leave the greedy white men with their problems. *(Shaking his head)* I've heard about stealing goats, chickens, or even sheep, but who ever hear 'bout stealing people? An' all these people they stealing, what they goin' to do with them?

(Instantly, the men are startled by a human voice sounding like a bird, whistling a kind of signal, near them. Jabari jumps to his feet, signals for quiet with his finger on lips)

JABARI Trouble coming! Take cover! *(Whispering, he signals to the two men separately without speaking)*

JABARI *(With hand gestures he points to Seth):* You go left. *(To Abi)* You take the right. *(Pointing to himself)* I'll go and see what it is. *The two men hide behind trees like shadows, and Jabari wastes no time in jumping into a thick bush, not fearing whatever is in there. There's a violent scuffle with someone grunting in the hidden bushes followed by a scream, then an eerie silence).*

A VOICE Ahh!!! Ahh!!! Ahh!!! *(The voice fades)*
(Jabari emerges from the bushes alone, covered in blood.

JABARI *Staring coldly into Abi's eyes he wipes a bloodied knife on his sleeve)* Now, as I was saying, **all** threats mus' be eliminated.

SETH & ABI *(Looking fearful)* But what was it, sah?

JABARI *(sneering):* **What** was it? You mean **who** was it? And whoever that was, is in the bush they now quite dead!

SETH & ABI What?! Dead, sah!

JABARI As I was saying, I've a plan for the final raid. Go home now. We meet here early tomorrow morning for the collection. You have enough time to think 'bout the money we'll be counting – riches, brothers, riches!

(Jabari laughs out loudly, punching his fist in the air)
[Exit Seth and Abi

JABARI   *(Contemplating his actions)*

This easy job of stealing people for the white man, can't be good, but on the other hand, can't be bad either. First of all, it'll free me from the burden of becoming a *Sangoma* or *bush medicine man*. Trouble is, my father didn't ask me if I wanted to do anything else in my life. I have my *own* ambitions. And I must break from their mould of thinking the first- born have to walk in his father's footsteps. I will break this by showing them I can make my own money; become rich, without their help. Then, perhaps they'll understand that a man really don't always have to follow traditions and and all those old, old traditional customs. Plus, my destiny is *not* to remain here; there is a world out there to discover. I've a glimpse of what it would be like, to be free from our stifling beliefs; living a life that others only dream of having themselves.

Look at my father's life – a popular *Sangoma*, strangled by traditions; Stuck in one stupid place and constantly bogged down night and day, with people's problems, persistently giving advice, making bush medicine, no enjoyment in life; no time for me either! Instead, he puts up with a limited life of doing things for other people, who can't pay him properly for what he does anyway!

Of course, he'll be disappointed; *if* he ever finds out I was involved in stealing African people for the white man. But how will he know that? Most people won't dare open their mouths. After all, I'm his Son and he's their saviour, they need him more, than to go and talk badly about me.

(Rises from his seat and stretches)

Well, their foolish proverb say, *"Don't count your chickens before they hatch!"* (Stupes loudly). S-T-U-P-E-S! Me, I counting mine right now! I know that by the end of

tomorrow, I'll be the richest, young man around, and that is pretty good enough reason for me to carry out the kidnap raid. *(He shrugs and laughs loudly)*
And it's *my* life, *my* future, *my* business; so, come what may!

[Exit Jabari

ACT 1 SCENE 3 – THE CONSIPIRACY

SETTING - *(Seth and Abi are in a reflective mood, sitting on a bench near to Seth's home)*

- **ABI**   Look man, ah sorry about earlier today. Jabari is a nice guy but he seems too jumpy these days. In fact, if he wasn't my good friend from way back, I would say he's losing his damn mind! That paranoia is getting worse every day. The man doesn't trust his own shadow nowadays! And yet we're called *Hunters of the Shadow;* living in the shadows of the forest, hunting people!
- **SETH**   Mmm, proverb say, *"If you put out cocoa, you must look for rain."* Hard to trust the son of a *Sangoma* I'd say. If he don't trust people, why should *we* trust him?
- **ABI**   What you mean?
- **SETH**   Well, his father has power. Together, they could use it to take our share of the money and then make us run mad!
- **ABI**   *(Shaking his head in agreement)*
  Yeah, you mean like a double-crossing us and then putting the all the blame on us?
- **SETH**   *(He nods)* You trust him? Look, Jabari alone is dealing with the white men. Do you know what they talking about? What if he really trying to undercut us with them? We don't know if he telling us the truth about the full amount of money they paying. How much is he really getting?
- **ABI**   *(Shrugs)* So what you saying? He's holding out on us?
- **SETH**   Well, I took the liberty of asking Mr. Murphy to meet us right here; in fact, he should be here any minute now.
- **ABI**   What! How come you know the white man personally?
- **SETH**   Look, we're all *Hunters of the Shadow*, the two white devils deal with all of us behind each other's back. How else they will get this huge amount of people they looking for?
- **ABI**   *(Nodding)* I see, I see!
- **SETH**   Here he comes now. *(Whispers)* Let me do the talking, I've a plan for the two of us.

(Enter Mr. Murphy – a white Hunter of the Shadow; looking over his shoulder suspiciously)

MURPHY *(Acting cagily)* OK, so you say you got something for me?

SETH Evening sah! My friend here raided more than 5 villages and we have good news for you. We have seventy-five people now, ready and waiting for transport; that is, if you want to deal with us separately, from Jabari.

MURPHY You have 75 people, but I can raise your price, if you can bring me 100 people by tomorrow, latest.

ABI But sah, we have 75 people for you; 15 more than Jabari was offering you.

MURPHY Yes, but can you bring me what I ask? If you can, I'll give you double Jabari's price. But I'm no time-waster, you hear me! You people like to waste time, either under-cutting each other, or cutting each other's throat! My ship sails in 2 days time. Bring me 100 people and you have a deal!

SETH We'll bring you exactly what you ask, sah. *(Sounding triumphant)* And as a bonus, we'll give you one extra – *free of charge!*

ABI It's a very, very good *bonus*, sah!

MURPHY OK, you people can do what you want, just bring me no less than 100 people tomorrow, by 4pm sharp. Or Jabari would get to know about this little deal with you behind his back, and it won't be my fault!

SETH Oh no sah, no need for that, we have transport waiting. We'll meet you at the harbour, 4pm sharp, sah!

[Exit Murphy

ABI *(Whispering)* Listen Seth, ah have another master plan. Tomorrow, we'll go with Jabari to his drop-off point at 6pm.

SETH That'll give us enough time to do our own drop-off first; without him getting suspicious.

ABI When we make the drop-off with Jabari, we'll hold him down and tranquilise him with his own *Sangoma* bush medicine. Then we'll throw him in, with the rest of the white man's pile.

SETH Yes, he'll be one of the people going away with the white devils. *(Rubbing his hands with glee).* We'll take our share of the money, Jabari's share, and then we'll get away with it, scotch free!

ABI *(They snigger in delight)* So, when he wake up, he'll be far away from here, and from us!

SETH Man, that is a master plan! *(They laugh out loudly)* C'm on, man, let's do this!

BOTH MEN *(Singing and dancing jubilantly, in call-and-response style)*

>No white man go catch me, oh!
>*No, no white man go catch me!*
>No white man go catch me, oh!
>*No, no white man go catch me!*
>
>No white man go catch me, oh!
>*No, no white man go catch me!*
>No white man go catch me, oh!
>*No, no white man go catch me!*

[Exeunt

ACT 1 SCENE 4 – NAMING CEREMONY INTERRUPTED

STAGE DIRECTION: *Curtains opens on stage revealing a group of people in a festive mood, celebrating in a family home; a Babalawo (Ifa Priest), a beautifully dressed mother, father, grandparents, friends and a 7-day old baby, gathered for a Yoruban naming ceremony. Happy African high-life music is playing, people are chatting, congratulating the parents and admiring the baby. They bring gifts. Then the Baba, dressed in white, holds up his hand for silence, signalling the start of the ceremony. The music fades then stops.*

(*A Babalawo is standing in front the gathered group smiling*)
BABALAWO Welcome, one and all, to this **Esen'taye,** our naming ceremony. First of all, special ancestral blessing on my brother, Oladepo Obasango, Senior of this house and father of this child. (*He points to the baby on the mother's lap*)
FATHER (*The Father nods*) Welcome *Baba!*
BABALAWO Also blessing to the woman sitting next to him, his queen-wife, Elerie Obasango, the beautiful mother, who is holding the seed of her womb, (*pointing to the baby in mother's arms*); the beautiful baby we are going to name today.
MOTHER (*She nods*) Welcome *Dadi!*
BABAWALO I also give an extra special welcome to the witnesses present here; the strong lineage of grandparents, other family members and their friends too. As you know, naming a baby is a lot more than just giving it a name.
GROUP (*Varied responses*):
VOICE That's right!
VOICE Yes Baba!
VOICE Amen!
BABALAWO Today, this ceremony will determine the entire destiny of this child because we believe a child lives out the meaning of his name. That's why we have these 7

symbolic items to express the hope of a successful life for this baby.
(The Babawalo moves closer to the table and holds up each item as he speaks)
Firstly, we have water here: **Water** is everlasting, it has no enemies, and everything in life needs water to survive. We will give it, so this child will never be thirsty in life and no enemies will slow his growth. Next is this one, **Palm oil** or **epo**: We will give this child for a smooth and easy life; and living a life in love and no friction. Not forgetting our special **Kola nut** or **obi:** We will give this child to repel the evil in life. We believe that **Peppe** or **Ata,** with its many seeds, we give it a fruitful life, with lots of children. And there is **Honey** or **Oyin:** We give it so that it will bring this child a sweet and happy life. This next one is......................

The Babawalo's speech is loudly and abruptly interrupted in mid-stream. There is loud shouting as a vehicle draws up outside the house. Fierce, angry, black, and white armed men, barge in and everyone is forced to scatter. They create a scuffle, and unleash physical violence, resulting in havoc. There is grabbing, beating, screaming, and arrests of all the able-bodied occupants of the house; young men and young women are violently handled.

BABALAWO Eh-jah! What happen! How dare you come here and...............? *(He is beaten with big sticks and sharp blades, as are all the old men and women)*

YOUNG MAN Shut up now, old man! Who say you can talk? *(He hits the Baba again, who falls to the ground).*

MEN'S VOICE *(Pointing to young people in the crowd)* You! Come with me, and you, and you too! Get outside now! *(He chooses those he takes, yelling and beating them with a large stick as he forces them outside the house. They are dragged by other helpers and thrown into* *waiting trucks outside. There is chaos and confusion).*

MAN BOARDING TRUCK *(Points threateningly to the crowd)* We comin' back for the rest of you. Talk to anyone, and you're all dead!

(Mixed voices of young people wailing, as they are being forced outside from parents)

VOICE 1 Ah! No! Why! Mama, Why! What's happening? Please save me!

VOICE 2 No, stop it! Somebody help me! What's happening? Mama!!

VOICE 3 Save me! I don't want to go! Please, help me, somebody! Mama!

MOTHER'S VOICE Gang-Gang, my daughter! Leave my chile! Woeeh! Please leave my daughter *(She throws herself on the ground).*

GANG-GANG Mama! Mama! Help me! Mama! Please! Help me, mama! Don't let them take me, Ma-ma! Please! Please! Ma-ma!

MOTHER'S VOICE Why? Why? Give me back my child, Gang Gang! Somebody help her, Please! Gang-Gang! Woeeh!

GANG-GANG *(Voice fades in the distance, as the truck drives away)* Ma-ma! Ma-ma! Help me! Ma-ma! Please! Help me, mama! Don't let them take me, Ma-ma!

(There is a cacophony of distressful wailing, shouting, and crying among those who remain; after the gang drives off with the kidnapped youngsters. The screaming children's voices echo and fade, as the truck disappears; then there is silence!)

ANANCY To destroy the sovereignty of a people, you must first destroy their <u>name</u>. This is directly linked to their history, their culture, their psychological well-being; in fact, their total cultural Identity!…………….

(Solo with backing men's chorus singing)

        ⁺Shosholoza
        Shosholoza
        Kulezontaba
        Wen uyabalaka
        Kulezontaba
        Stimelasipume'e
        Shosholoza
        Shosholoza
        Kulezontaba
        Wen uyabalaka
        Kulezontaba

(Silence as the lighting fades and curtains close)
                                                    [Exeunt

⁺ *See* **Glossary** *for song translation*

ACT 1 SCENE 5 – THE PROPHECY

STAGE DIRECTIONS: African Drumming as *Curtain Opens, showing a split setting. People are gathered at one end (Babalawo and Elders) and Anancy at the other end. The stage is dark, the only stage lighting, red spot lights – one over the house gathering so they seem like a silhoette and the other over Anancy. The spot light brightens to white light when they speak.*

ANANCY You see that! And so it was that Africa's peace, was forever interruped, even to this day. The peaceful Continent was hijacked by a disease of pandemic proportions, that infected Africa's land with a rude awakening. That infection was the kidnapping by white men, of African people; able-bodied, strong men and women who had tilled the soil, and lived in peace with families and neighbours. And while parts of that great Continent enjoyed natural riches, there were those who were selling their brothers and sisters. Seemingly, they had became infected by the same evil disease – greed and avarice, from the *White Hunters of the Shadow*. Imagine, their triangular trade; a movement of stolen people from Africa, taken to the Caribbean to work on plantations. There they would work to produce sugar, which is then taken to Europe; spear-headed by Britain, France, Spain, and Holland to build and expand those countries' wealth.

(Spotlight fades over Anancy)

[Exit Anancy

STAGE DIRECTIONS: (*The spotlight changes back to red and silhoette over Anancy and switches to the cameo at the other end of the stage, with the Elders and a Babalawo Chief discussing. Candles are lit and the men stand in a circle with background drumming, as they prepare to comunicate with their African Gods. They move in a circular motion, grunting. The women, dressed in red dresses with* *red head-ties, are singing and dancing in the background, as accompaniment. Drumming quietens then men begin to speak.*

ELDERS *(Looking upwards and holding their open hands, they take turns to speak)*

ELDER 1 Oh *Orofi* Olodumare, High God, hear us; Ogun, Oya, Obatala, Yemaya; hear us our heart is so sore, draw near!

ELDER 2 Oh Shango, Elegba and Papa Eshu, God of the crossroad in our life, we ask you to come. With great humility, Oh Great spirit, we come before you all and implore your intercession. Hear our petition.

EDDER 3 We, your children, are broken. Big evil white snakes are roaming our lands stealing our precious chickens. Our nests grow empty daily, and our heart's full of pain. We call on you Elegba to remove all obstacles; Shango, give us power over our enemies; Obatala, bring peace and Ogun, fight our attackers.

BABALAWO CHIEF For as long as our children are scattered around the world, I curse those who have come here, stolen our children and divided our land. We will defeat all those responsible for this tragedy here, with great calamities of wars, suffering and cruelty, for as many generations as it will take; whether we're alive or called home early by the great Olodumare but one day, our children will be free to return to this soil.

ELDERS TOGETHER Listen to us *Shango*! Help us *Yemaya*! Don't forsake us *Ogun*! Intercede for us *Ellegua*! Hear us *Oshun*! Look at us with favour *Obatala*! Act with favour for us *Oya*! Grant what we ask, through the *Seven African Powers*. Orofi, bless us that we and those who are stolen from Africa, may be forever blessed wherever they go.
Immediately, thunder cracks and lighting flashes (Shown by the intermittent changing of the different spot lights above) A God's thunderous loud voice is heard speaking.

OLODUMARE SPEAKS Wipe your tears my hurting people. Take comfort that your prayers have been heard. The war will be very long and the journey will be hard, but we will not forsake you. Wherever our people wander, *The Seven Powers* will be there, fighting with and for them, from inside their hearts and minds. Know, that we have commanded the God Ananse to travel with them. But She will be in disguise, living inside each and every one of them; armed with the wisdom that will help them defeat the White devils.
(Drumming as the men and women joined by Anancy war-Dance and leave the stage, except Anancy)

ANANCY The time has come for me, as **Ananse,** to go as spider undercover. Of all the creations in the world, Nyame chose me. Armed with a great mission because
I'm the smartest, I'm the cleverest, the bravest of all;
To go about the face of this earth as wisdom incognito!
So if you feeling really smart, it's me Anancy inside you,
If you hear good wisdom, just take it and bring it home.
I carry enough wisdom inside these eight arms and legs.
This way, I can make sure I spread wisdom everywhere.
So I will ride on the waves with the crying slaves on the ships, that will sail the Atlantic ocean, to prevent their destruction. I will hide among my people, witnessing atrocities in the land, in order to tell you my stories about life in the Caribbean; Because I, the ***new Anancy***, mek it so! Yes, I mek it so!

[Exit Anancy

ACT 2 SC. 1 - STOLEN CHILDREN LEAVE AFRICA

STAGE DIRECTION: *At a Harbour, young people are being led into a boat, some crying, limping, coughing, wailing. Gang-Gang is badly bruised but defiant. She tries to kick, lashes out and bites the Hunter who grabs her ear. Her clothes are torn. The kidnapped group is being handed over to the White Hunters as the last African destination.*

MURPHY *(Pointing to Gang-Gang)* So what happened to this one! She's damaged? You beat her too bad.

ABI Sorry boss, we had too much trouble from this one. She keeps running away, we had to stop twice to catch her. She seems to have some special powers, that one!

SETH Yeah, like this one is a winch, we put double ropes on her and still can't understand how she keeps getting away! She must be a winch.

GANG-GANG *(She's pushed from behind by Seth, so she hisses, bares her teeth and kicks him)* Take that, you dirty dog!

SETH *(Attempts to slap Gang-Gang in retaliation):* You little ………!

MURPHY *(Interrupts)* Stop it, man! I pay you for good stock. What am I going to do with damaged people, who won't survive the long journey ahead?

GANG-GANG *(Looking at the men defiantly, attempts to break Free, muttering)* Hey! I curse you, I curse you all! Fire, on your families! Fire, on your lives! Fire on Everything!

ABI *(Whispers to Seth)* They need to watch this one and put her in a strong-hold. She's going to be real trouble. They might have to sedate her, like that greedy one we tranquilised and put in the bag, on board the ship.

(The two men struggle as she fights them in a combat but they manage to overcome the defiant Gang-Gang and put her on board the ship)

MURPHY *(Abi to Seth whilst rubbing his hands together)* That's all then, everyone accounted for?

ABI Yes sah, in total it's 101 - we said we would give you an extra one - he is free, sah! Good to do business with sah!

JEFFREY Such generosity! *(Shaking both men's hands)* OK, nice doing business with you too!
(To his colleague) Mr. Murphy, I believe our business here in Africa is done, for the time being, at least. *(He sighs)*

MURPHY I'd definitely say so; then all aboard! Let's get all hands on deck. We set sail.

*[**Exeunt**_*

(The kidnapped children are all on board a ship, distraught, crying, coughing and wailing. The ship's horn is sounded)

GANG-GANG *(Sings)*
I cannot let you go, my love, Oh Africa,
I just don't know how I shall ever exist;
Without you guiding my steps, my peace:
You have a big place in my heart for sure,
My soul's tied to you, this land and shore.
Hear me Ancestors of our land and sea,
Watch over Africa and watch over me.
I go, not knowing where on earth I'll be,
So, if I die my love, with all this misery
Here let my bleeding heart find eternal rest;
Then I'll pray an everlasting sleep, my love,
To return to you when my soul is set free,
For one more time to be with you, my love;
Farewell my Africa, Farewell my love.
Farewell my Africa, Farewell my love.

*[**Music fades**_*

ANANCY And so this *'bleeding heart'* of Gang-Gang, symbolised the *'bleeding'* state of Africa – losing its sons and daughters to countries of men with great might. Forcefully wrenched from the Cradle of Civilisation, greedily ravaged by exploiters; men who manipulated their dark minions, hungry to eat, with deceit and denied people their basic Human Right. Then took part in a trading business, using a Slave Triangle – ***From Africa to the Caribbean, then from there to Britain, and back to Africa again*** – with a vision to force, rape, pillage and poach people from their peace, to work on plantation in a new land. Master. Coloniser. Thief!

[Exeunt

(Drumming as Anancy leaves the stage)

ACT 2 SCENE 2 - MIDDLE PASSAGE CROSSING LAMENT

SETTING: *On board the Slave Ship, rough seas, high winds, fear is all around. Gang-Gang defies the raging storm and calls on the Orishas.*

JEFFREY *(To Murphy)* This storm seems relentless. Been watching The ship for some time. She's like a bucking horse, thrashing around like a violent animal.

MURPHY Looks like the time to sound the alarm! Tonight could be our Waterloo.
(Ship's bell rings, men with hurried movements dash from bow to stern).

JEFFREY Summon the children to rise! Bring them up from the hold.
(Cries from frightened children, as the ship rises like a towering mountain, and the angry wind rages. Children look skywards, trying to hold on as best they can, to remain steady and secure)

VOICE   Save me Oh!

VOICE   Oh Mama! Please, somebody help us, Oh!

VOICE   Eh-ja, **Yemaya**, Help us Oh!
(Standing, chained, wet, defiant, unafraid, Gang-Gang calls on the African Orishas, (Ogun, Legba, Eshu and Obatala) She faces the 4 compass points in turn, as she speaks)

GANG-GANG Oh **Ogun**, have you come to save us? Listen, we are hidden here. Can you see us **Legba**? What is this trickery? **Eshu**, are we to meet you at this watery crossroad? Here, in this junction that's a watery grave, with angry marine gods, calm this ferocious storm and give us a peaceful way out of this wet hell. **Obatala,** speak against the unleased rage on the white devils, who keep us chained here to die with him. I promise to remember you all my days, after this journey ends, by giving my life in service to you all – just save me please!

Save us, please!   **(Storm subsides)**
(Anancy enters to comment on the action)

ANANCY The sea was a split-personality marine god, unleasing its rage on the injustice of the innocents. Yet it would be wrong to take them as victims, in the target against the White Hunters, in this night of torment. Like mountains, the waves rose, then fell, smashing the ship sideways, spewing salt-water like an angry tom-cat. It thrashed the ship around like a battering ram against the hull, as the bitter winds roared unrepentantly. Water towered skyward, causing the ship to fall like a toy into the salty foaming brine. The night was dark and stormy, as the wind howled wildly. How many were lost? It was hard to tell. But some children - dead cargo, thrown overboard the next morning, were those found twisted, restricted by their shackles; linked one to the other; as they scrambled for safety overnight. The night's Angel of Death, may have called them home, to spare them from the horrors yet to come! We are many different peoples speaking in different tribal languages, but we are all one African nation. Only time will tell what is to become of us here.

[Exit Anancy

(On board the Ship: Mr. Jeffrey to Mr. Murphy, the morning after the stormy night)

JEFFREY Last night was a very bad night. How many did we lose?

MURPHY I'd say roughly around 20% of our cargo!

JEFFREY What! 20%? Are you sure? This trip is a financial loss! We can't afford to lose any more, and they need to be in good shape for the onward sale. Bring them up for exercise! Lifeless cargo is no good to us.

MURPHY *(Yawning and rubbing his eyes)* I doubt they'd have the energy to exercise. Like us, they were up pretty much all night, in the storm.

JEFFREY *(Looking annoyed):* Look, whip them if you have to, but wake them up now! Get them all on deck for exercise.

We have to get them looking like saleable goods; can't afford to have half-dead cargo, when we arrive. Otherwise, no one would want to buy them from us!

MURPHY *(Shaking his head, disappointedly)* This journey's turning out to be a bad luck one, not like the others. Another storm like this and we're done for! Let's go and calculate the loss.

[Exit Jeffrey & Murphy

(Sound of whip cracking and children's voices crying out from being whipped in turn)

VOICES No! Stop!
VOICES Ah! No!
VOICES Aw! Aw!
ADULT VOICE Jump! Skip! Dance! Limbo!
ANANCY Forged from the slave-ship experience, so it is our limbo dance was born – a bittter-sweet memory of expression today, of what it was like to be a slave, on board a slave-ship. This dance saved and kept slaves alive, as forced, physical exercise. Today, we dance it to show off and compete with one another in entertainment!
(Anancy sings - Dancers limbo to steelpan music)
I want a man to limbo like me,
Limbo, limbo like me –
I want a man to limbo like me,
Limbo, limbo like me –
I want a woman to limbo like me,
Limbo, limbo like me –
I want a woman to limbo like me
Limbo, limbo like me.

[Exit Anancy

ACT 3 SCENE 1 - ARRIVAL DAY IN THE CARIBBEAN

SETTING: *The front of a 18th century house of grandeur, built by the Plantation owner; the home of Peter Bristol, his wife and teenage twins – a boy and girl. Known as the 'Great House,' the building is a gated mansion painted in white, with many windows, high ceilings, polished wooden floors and a wide veranda. Attached to this house are a boiling house, stables and outbuildings. A man dressed in white, wearing a wide-brimmed hat is standing in front of the house, with 2 strong, profusely sweating black men on either side of him. They are wearing torn working-clothes and each holding a cutlass.*

STAGE DIRECTION: *Trucks, loaded with a group of mixed-gendered young slaves pull up in front of a Great House. The slaves' hands are tied with ropes and linked to each other; they look bewildered, hungry and exhausted. The man, with a straw hat, dressed in white is immediately greeted by both Jeffrey and Murphy, who jump out of the trucks to reet and speak to him.*

JEFFREY *(To Peter Bristol with a strong hand-shake)*: We made it! A journey from hell, but we're here at last, with a good crop of breeders, as requested; young, strong and easy to shape into your way of doing things here.

PETER BRISTOL Well, I'm glad to see you both with the goods. There's much work here and we need all the pairs of their hands we can get. This sugar plantation estate is huge with hard work; we need quality workers that won't die under the strain.

MURPHY *(Moving towards Peter to shake his hand)* I think with these young ones, your investment will bear fruit, *literally*, for years to come. *(He laughs wryly)* Let's just say this crop has a longer life expectancy, than the older ones; great yield and return on investment. *(Averting his eyes from Peter Bristol)* Though we have a slightly reduced cargo now, than anticipated, because of sea storms and some fatal sickness on board, but I would say on the whole, these young

    breedable ones, in time, will make up for the
    initial stock shrinkage.
PETER BRISTOL *(Motioned to the two black Handlers and pointing to the slaves)*
    Get some help and take the stock into the outbuildings, and stay there with them until I come with paperwork.
THE MEN Yess, Boss! Right away, Boss!
PETER BRISTOL *(Gestures to Murphy and Jeffrey)*
    Shall we go and deal with the paperwork inside?

             [Exeunt

ANANCY Stranded here on this emerald shore, called **Tobago**, where blue skies beckon greetings to our hapless group and the green land waves its welcome in the luscious branches, that rise and fall with soft breezes; is the fireball overhead in a cloudless sky. It is an end to the watery world their spirits had fought hard to survive in. This warm breeze is a healing balm to their dry, lack-lustre skin and down-pressed souls. Today is the first time I have seen my young people smile. Their cries at the *Land Ahoy!* announcement were cries of hope and expectations, of joy and relief, of pain and loss of their families. Today's day and date I do not know but, I Anancy, witnessed when Africa's stolen children whispered thanks to their Orishas, who had not forgotten, but escorted them in their prayers to this land. What lies ahead they really don't know! Here is their New World, an alternative, a place of promise, paradise; a land for reconstruction, preservation, adoption and renewal. It's a place where from today, I'm no longer **Akan Ananse,** but become ***Anancy the spider, a trickster in the Caribbean;*** filled with wisdom to help my people outwit and rebel against their slave masters. Among them I will hide, tasked with this new role, to lead and guide, as directed by Olodumare. Ssssshhhh!!

          [Exit Anancy
          Mournful music plays

ACT 3 SCENE 2 - FIRST DAY PLANTATION WOES

SETTING - *Outside Slave Quarters. Slaves being branded and re-named, are put to work on the plantation, assigned to genderised jobs. The male slaves join the experienced men in learning how to plant and cut cane. The young females are taken by older women, who will train them to serve, cook, clean, and some to gather cane alongside children slaves.*

SLAVE MANGER *(In front of the gathered slaves and pointing to a Black Slave handler)* Gather the group for branding and naming; line them up one by one, over there!

SLAVES *(Crying out loudly, one by one, they are branded with hot irons; they fall to the ground – convulsing violently in shock)* Ahh! Haaaaa! Awu! Ah!! Kai! Oh-oh!

WHITE MANAGER *(Arrives on a horse, wielding a whip, shouts for the slaves to form into different groups)*
Take the men on this side!
(He cracks the whip on a female slave, who instantly falls to the ground, then whips others. Pointing to Gang-Gang and slinging his whip towards her)
You, over there with the others! Faster, faster! Now!

GANG-GANG *(Gang–Gang with the speed of lightning, grabs the whip immediately with great force, so he falls off his horse. With skillful manoevures she wrestles him to the ground then stands over him with her foot on his head, and scowls at him).* I tell you to stop that right now; see, it hurts, yeh!
(With wildness in her eyes, and baring teeth, she growls at the white manager, then lifts her foot off his head).
See, how this one hurt, same way you hurt me, and what for, eh? *(She yells at the Black Slave Manager)* You too, I say stop it, right now!

SLAVES *(Loud gasps and shouts in astonishment are heard from the surrounding slaves)*
Eh-Eh! Haaaaaa!! Yeparipa!! Kai!! Ah-ree!
E-hen! This one is winch, oh! Poh-shay!

There's fear in the slaves' eyes as they clap their hands in despair, some put them on their heads in disgust and disbelief, at Gang Gang's daring display with the white slave manager. Stunned by the surprised attack, he brushes off his shame and game-like, he stalks Gang-Gang, by walking around her, and squaring up to her as his prey.

WHITE MANAGER Well, well well! What have we here? This little frisky one spells BIG trouble.
(He orders the Black Slave assistant-handlers).
Take the others to the field now! This one *(pointing to the defiant Gang-Gang),* Bring her to me. I will teach her a lesson she'll never forget; the first lesson about obeying on this plantation. *(Embarrassed, he sneers and laughs out loudly)* She'll never forget it!

[Exits

SLAVES *(Older slaves gasp in horror, pointing at Gang-Gang)*
Eh-Eh! What is this? The Devil bring a winch here !
(Gasps followed by whispers and recoil from children slaves)

FEMALE SLAVE *(Pregnant and slightly older than Gang-Gang, a female slave intervenes)*
My sister, please listen, there's a time for everythin' out here. A time to speak and a time to say yes; time to play foolish; time to fight back; but my sis, that time is definitely not now! I tell you, it's *not* now!

GANG-GANG I'm Gang-Gang, warrior woman, trained to combat and protect, and not to tolerate this. O pari o! It's finished. I mean it too!

FEMALE SLAVE *(Taking the young Gang-Gang by the hand).*
Yes, you new and you young. You strong like a young stallion but the Sister is right. I was like you when I firs' came here but see, *(She points to her right foot with 3 toes).* Look at me foot, I lost 2 toes for fightin' back. Each time I run away and fight back, they cut off one of me toes. So I had to learn to fight in another way, to stay alive. Let me teach you how to prepare herbs. This land is full of

medicine; good medicine and bad medicine. You need to learn how to use them to your advantage. *(Tapping her on the shoulder)* Come Sis, now's the time to learn how to survive in this land. *(Shaking her head)* It's *not* the time to fight; not without traditional armour.

GANG-GANG *(Angrily)* Haaaaaa!! You people not fightin' back! Why? Where are your warriors?

FEMALE SLAVE *(Talking back angrily to Gang-Gang)*
Kai! Fight back? You jus' come here, leh me tell you somethin', you have no power over these people? They beat you, you run, they catch you! You work hard like a man and they rape you in front of others. Yes, you bawl, you scream, where's your power over them? *(Pointing to the pregnant slave among them).* Look at her, where's her power over her own body? Tell me, isn't it *their* seed inside her? They breed us like animals. You mus' learn to use some other power to overcome this ugly hell we're *all* trapped in. Learn! You mus' go back into your mind and remember what you already know – African medicine, African religion, African mind, and African ways of thinking. Use the knowledge that you know, you hear me, chile! Proverb say, *"There's more than one way so skin a cat!"*

[Exits

GANG-GANG *(Angry and defiant)* One thing I know is how to fight and protect, to hunt, and to keep my tribe, with my militia warrior women; death has no fear for me!

FEMALE SLAVE Gobsa! Listen eh, expect to get a real bad beating today, oh! They'll not feed you and you'll be buried in a hole in the ground up to your neck, in the blazing hot sun, all day; without a head-covering; and that's *after* he has his own way with you first. Some people don't come out of this alive; especially as this is your firs' day here. But if the 96 degrees sun and Massah rape punishment doh kill you today, then Eshu is with you. That means, in this your crossroads with Death, he'll save you and tell you what you mus' do when Death comes to claim you. If Death rejects you, then Eshu has a special job here for you, if he doesn't reject you, then we will be burying you at sundown. Chile, just prepare your mind for the big painful, test that's coming! *(Shaking her head, she taps her on her shoulder, in a consolatory way)*

[Exits

GANG-GANG *(Defiantly she crouches low in a combative position, as if she is staking out her prey, then make warrior dance moves that displays fighting routines, and appearing confident as she shows readiness for the impending 'combat' that she's being warned against)*

A HOUSE SLAVE *(Identified by her better style of dress, a house slave approaches, pointing to the remaining group of slaves)*

You, you and you, come with me, house work is too much for me today oh. I have cooking and cleaning work for you. I will show you what to do. You will work inside the Great House, with me today only. One mistake around the massah and his missis or children, and you might not live to see the next day. Watch me closely - walk like me, speak like me, never look them in the eye; you will learn to have power like me – the power to feed them in order for them to stay alive! They think that they have all the power – yes, maybe the power to control us with the whip and force themselves on us for sex, but we have power too! Come with me, I will show you how to use it.

[Exits

(Enter a black slave handler followed by male slaves, whom he addresses).

BLACK HANDLER My advise to you young men is to stick close by me. I will put you to work alongside mature men to learn what to do. Follow them, learn their every move. We work from sun-up to sun-down cutting cane, alongside women and children. Look out for each other, some of you might faint, some of you might die in the heat, others will need to carry dead bodies from the cane field. Expect to be beaten, when the white massah feels like it. Massah, wants cane cutting, he wants cane pressed, he wants cane crushed, he wants cane boiled. We make molasses and sugar. Massah is always in a hurry to get more, and more, and .....

WHITE MANAGER *(Re-enters and interrupts the Black slave handler)*
What are you all still doing here? Get to work at once! Or I'll.....
(As he raises his whip, he notices Gang-Gang then stops).
I told you to bring *this one* to me. Do it, now!
(He rides around the compound and gets off his horse, behind a row of slave shacks).

BLACK HANDLER *(Nods to the group of men to follow him. As he leads them towards the Plantation Estate. He breaks into a song, in the call-and-response style)*
Call - *Let's go to work and cut the cane,*
Response - *Let's go to work and cut the cane!*
Call - *We go to work and plant the cane,*
Response - *We go to work and plant the cane!*
Call - *There's plenty sun but it might rain,*
Response - *There's plenty sun but it might rain!*

Voices fade

[Exeunt

ACT 3 SCENE 3 – GANG-GANG'S RECOVERY

SETTING: *Inside a mature female slave cabin. Gang-Gang has been rescued from her near-death punishment and is being nursed back to consciousness by other slaves. The women are healing Gang-Gang by African traditional ritual. The room is filled with burning herbs, two candles - one at Gang-Gang's head and the other at her feet. Beads are used for the prayers the women utter over Gang-Gang and a small bundle of green leaves is used to sprinkle the specially prepared water over her.*

GANG-GANG *(Half-conscious and delirious)* Ah! Ah! No! No! Please, Stop! Mama! Where is my Ma-ma? I want Ma-ma!

MATURE SLAVE *(Whispering, as she dips the bunch of leaves in the water and shakes it over the severely ill Gang-Gang)* Shh! Child, you'll cause more trouble, if anyone finds us doing this here. We put you here to nurse you back to life.

A SLAVE *(Softly singing a prayer on her knees, with the beads in her hand)*

O here we are, my spirits, come and tell us what to do with this your chile, Gang-Gang. Eshu sent her back here from the crossroads. Tell us what to do to keep her alive. *(She shakes a rattle repeatedly over the sick girl and begins to speak as a male African voice directs her).*

SPIRIT VOICE *(A Male voice speaking remotely)*

Dry your tears mother. The brutality my daughter has suffered has torn her soul, but I will restore her in 3 days. In the spirit world we recognise this warrior, called Gang-Gang. Her name means, *"the one who will lead."* Though she may seem numb inside now, the healing spirits are already retrieving the broken parts of her soul; look for restoration in 3 days time.

[Exit Male Spirit Voice

MATURE SLAVE *(Whispering in the sick girl's ear)*
Here, drink chile, berry juice, mixed with leaves and bark; it's good for you. You proved to be worthy of the special mixture I put in it – the secret drink of the gods. From now on, it will make you unconquerable. It will give you more warrior power over the white devils. With this special preparation, you will rise without objection and will have widespread influence to lead and teach others. Your kind of strength and boldness must be nurtured, for *our* own good. In 3 days you will be strong. It's the will of Olodumare. *(Groaning from Gang Gang)* Shhhhh! Sleep now, stay well; we'll meet on this side of your crossroad, when you wake!

[Exeunt

ANANCY *(Enters the stage to comment)*
And so it is that, I Anancy, must walk among the people, reminding them of the importance of remembering the old traditions. I show them how to adapt their lives in this New World. What you see here today, is the survival instinct in action but inside each and everyone of them, is the foundation of survival strategies for overcoming the greatest threat to man's existence. In truth, it is maintaining their African spirituality. I Anancy, exist incognito, hiding and speaking to their minds in all their activities; when their spirits sink low or when they need caution or advice, guidance and defence.
(Pointing to the end of the stage).
Come with me, I will take you on a tour around a Slave hideout on this Sugar Plantation Estate, to see how Africa is being transplanted in the Caribbean; how it's kept alive. Yes man, we clever you know! We pass it on from the older to the younger generation, before they die off; then from younger to those yet unborn; establishing traditions that await them, for as long as our people exist in the world; away from the Motherland. Let's go quick, before someone catch us!

ACT 3 SCENE 4 – RISE TO PROMINENCE

SETTING: *It's night-time. The moon is full, in dark-blue stage lighting. After a hard day's work, slaves gather in the bushes beyond their slaves quarters, to pass the time and to perform various African activities in gatherings that are strictly forbidden. (African drumming is heard in a jovial environment)*

ANANCY *(Whispering to the audience)* Let's go an' spy on a secret in the woods. Ssshhh! Born in the heart of the Congo region of Central Africa, Kumina landed here in the Caribbean. Now a dance, but now the most African religious expression in the Caribbean since the 1800's. This dance survives because it is done secretly in the bushes, despite being forbidden by the Plantation owners. Used to inspire courage and bravery in the face of their danger and hardship, this dance ritual has a big role to play among the slaves. Wait, you will see how they try to maintain their sanity, instil hope and garner strength, heal individuals with various ailments with special medicinal help. But listen noh, the Plantation master disallowed slave gatherings of all kinds, beause he is afraid of rebellion and uprisings. The thing is, what *was* he really afraid of? The slaves other 'unknown' powers? And what was that? Witchcraft? Obeah? Religion? You *definitely* have to judge for yourselves. I goin' to dance in the corner over there, to remind me of my past self too! *(Sings)* "Over the moon and over the sea, I want to go, I want to...."

[Exit Anancy singing

GROUP *(Enter a group of women and men dancing the Kumina, led by Gang-Gang, and joined by younger slaves).*

GANG-GANG *(Leads as 'Queen' of the Kumina ritual, followed by a 'King' dancer from the group)*
Over the moon and over the sea
I want to go,
I want to go, I want to -
I want to go.
GROUP Over the moon and over the sea
I want to go,
I want to go, I want to -
I want to go.
GANG-GANG I want to go, I want to -
I want to go.
I want to go, I want to -
I want to go.
MATRIARCH *(Joins Gang-Gang in the dancing and commands)*
Bring the sick children! We healing them tonight.
CHILD *(Children are brought in the circle of dance. A child in brought in front with inflated stomach, is crying.)* Ai! Ai!Ai!
GANG-GANG Spin him round 3 times to the left and then spin him 3 times to the right. *(Trance-like, she dances around the child shouting)* You evil spirit, I say Go! Now! Get out of now! Now!
MATRIARCH Bring that one over there, with the sore leg, he can't walk but we transferring that sickness tonight!
(She dances around the old man in a frenzy)
GANG-GANG Those with headache, backache, toothache; all kinds of aches and pains, come into the centre. You have to learn how to move those aches and pains. Learn how to use your body, to heal your own body; control the spirit of pain and sickness. *(They all dance in a frenzy).*
MATRIARCH *(Leads whilst singing: Gang-Gang follows her, dancing in the ring).*
Over the moon and over the sea
I want to go
I want to go, I want to

        I want to go.
GROUP Over the moon and over the sea
        I want to go
        I want to go, I want to
        I want to go
GANG-GANG I want to go, I want to
        I want to go.
        I want to go, I want to
        I want to go.
        (Sounds of bird-like cawing is heard, from one of the strategic Lookouts; a planned signal to warn of impending danger.
A LOOK-OUT 1 *(Sounding urgent)* Caw-Caw! Caw-Caw!
A LOOK-OUT 2 *(Sounding urgent – deep gutteral grunts respond repeatedly to the cawing)* Caw-caw Grff! Caw-caw Grff!
A SLAVE Trouble comin', everybody run! Scatter now!

There's an instant end to their forbidden activity, after the signal of impending danger. All lights are put out. Quickly, they disperse groping their way in the dark, back to their slave quarters.

                                            *[**Exeunt**

ACT 3 SCENE 5 THE BIRTH ATTENDANT

SETTING: *Outdoor. Every-day life demands of Slaves on the Sugar Plantation Estate. Men and women slaves are cutting cane. Gang-Gang, the Plantation's Birth Attendant or Doula, is called to assist a woman who is in the process of advanced labour, in the cane field.*

(Running and panicking, towards Gang-Gang who's cutting cane with others)

ANA Help! Gang-Gang, help ma, you mus' come quick-quick!

GANG-GANG What! What happen?

ANA It's Mary, the baby comin' now! You mus' come, quick! She's down there; I t'ink she's dyin'! She's cryin' out for help, but they don't let us help her.

GANG-GANG Come quick! Whe' she is? Quick, let's go to her!
(Muttering to herself) I know this birth was too close, for her to be still doin' this hard, donkey-work, in a cane field. Last few days of pregnancy and still cuttin' and harvestin' cane like a man! Huh!
(She shakes her head, during the half-running pace to rescue Mary)

ANA *(Through tears)* She in a lot ah pain but Massah say he don't believe her. He t'inks she's lyin,' he say she mus' keep cuttin' cane. She keep fallin' down, too much pain but he keep whipin' her, sayin' she is just lazy. But I tell you that baby is really comin' – blood's everywhere!

GANG-GANG OK hush, hush! Let's just go quick-quick!
(They reach Mary, who is in advanced labour, lying helplessly on the ground. Gang-Gang kneels to attend to her)

SLAVE MANAGER *(Galloping, poised with his whip, he stops near the three women, then pointing to Gang-Gang)*
Well, well, if it's not miss warrior come back alive! You back for more! Get back to work now! Or you'll get more than what you had before. Worse than that one lying there!

GANG-GANG *(Unafraid, defiant, she turns to the slave manager as she is looked on by other slaves)*
Eh-Eh! Well, well, if it's not the devil himself! So you think beatin' a pregnant woman with a baby between her legs make you a big, bad boss! Why don't you come down from your big horse and go one-to-one with me, right here, now?
(She moves in a combative stance ready to tackle him)
Last time you were lucky! Now, is ready, ah ready for you!
(She spits on the ground in disgust, as she taunts him)

SLAVES *(Gasps of fear at Gang-Gang's confrontation, as some appeal to her to stop).*
Mammy, mammy, no! Will be more trouble, please don't!

GANG-GANG *(With hands on hips akimbo).* All-you askin' me to stop! That woman and child will die right now, if I don't help them! And I'm not lettin' that happen today. I'll fight him firs', then I'll save them! And this time he won't be so lucky with me!
(Turning to face the Slave Manager)
So, come down from your horse and fight me now, because I'm goin' to deliver that baby today! *(Encouraged by her bravery, angry slaves promptly leave their work, armed with work tools, crowd around Gang-Gang and the woman in child birth, to show their support).*

ELDER WOMAN *(Empowered, speaks to the women)* You two, Help Gang-Gang with Mary on the ground. *(To the men)* Face outwards and circle us, right 'round. C'm on, quick!

SLAVE MANAGER *(Being out-numbered by the rebellious show of force and the screams from Mary on the ground, he scowls at them, spurs his horse and rides off shouting)*
I'll be back in an hour, be done with this whore and this chirade! You must all get back to work!
[Exits

(Everyone assists in carrying the delicate Mary to a cabin for the birth).

GANG-GANG *(With quick succession of commands to women)* Ana, make lots of hot water and get some cloth. Put everything in this bucket. And you over there, take all these spices, pour everything in, quick-quick!
(Gang-Gang is frantic after touching Mary's stomach in strategic places)
She has less than 1 hour, there's some real problems here, because of the beatin' she got. Both mother and baby in big trouble. *(Shakes her head sadly at the other women)* Pray for no death today eh!
(Swiftly Gang-Gang searches for an amulet which she puts around Mary's leg, and smears white powdery substance all over her face)

A MATRIARCH Let's call Ogun, god of iron, to remove obstacles in this birth! *(Three women begin to shake beads and begin a prayer vigil, as they move in a circle in the corner whilst Gan-Gang tends to Mary)*

GANG-GANG *(Turning to Ana)* As young as you are, you seen too many mothers dyin' in child-birth on this Plantation. Too many babies dyin' when they're born. Maybe you could say our babies work like men on a plantation, even before they are born! That's why as *Doula*, I administer medicine to the raped girls, to prevent this type of situation from happenin'. It's the only power we have over our bodies, from being forced to breed like animals, in this livin' hell!

MARY *(Semi-conscious, with groans)* Ai! Ai! Ai! Ai!

GANG-GANG *(Examines Mary)* OK, Mary, now you're almost done, stay with us. You *must* stay with us, it's almost over. Please try to stay awake. You're almost there! Look, now stay with me, and push! C'm on now, push! There, you've done it!
(The newborn baby cries but there's grave concern for the mother, who is unconscious).

GANG-GANG I name this one, *Precious*.

>*(She looks at Mary's limped body and shakes her head in disappointment).*
>No more mother, but this little one is very precious to us now.
>*(She hands the baby to the elders)*

MATRIARCHS *(Receive the wrapped-up, crying baby)*
>We receive this little one called *Precious*.
>Thank you Ogun, for little *Precious!*

[Exeunt

ACT 4 SCENE 1: DINNER BOASTS

SETTING: *Inside the Great House of Peter Bristol, a Slave Trader and Plantation owner, around the dinner table. The Bristol family – (Peter, his wife Dora and 12yr old twins, Stella and Peter Junior), have guests to dinner; two nearby Plantation owners and their wives. There's commaraderie, a jovial mood among the gathering sitting around the table. Dinner is served by House slaves.*

ANANCY: Let me tell all-you something; some people just like to boast you see! Some boast about their conquests in love, while others boast about near-misses. But who ever heard about anyone actually boasting about buying and selling people? Yeah, you heard me right; buying people to feather their own nests. I mean big fat bank accounts; big, big houses, they call The Great House and ownership of millions of people! *(Shakes her head).*
And listen, talking about nests, come leh me show you a glimpse into some real fat-cats' lifestyle. You hear the saying *"Birds of a feather stick together?"* Well, these are like fat-birds in their comfortable nests; getting fatter and richer from the blood, sweat, tears and lives of the innocent people they trade in. Let's just zoom in on their conversation, to see how these lazy money-grabbers brag about their exploits. Listen well eh; they usually talk of nothing but sugar, making money and occasionally quarrelling over cockfighting, while they drink rum. Come closer – come, leh we see what happening. *(She moves towards the Dinner table and shouts out at them).*
What's the talk about today, fellas?

[Exits

PETER BRISTOL *(Standing with glass in hand)* Gentlemen, and of course, our gracious ladies too, I dare say; I would like to propose a toast, to our good fortune.

GUESTS *(Raising their glasses)* Hear! Hear! To our good fortune!

PETER BRISTOL *(Still on his feet)* In fact, I would like to propose another toast to our esteemed Royal African Company and her exclusive control of our trade; ivory, gold, dyewood, spices and slaves. *(He coughs then sits)*

ALL *(All raising their glasses to toast)* To the Royal African Company!

GUEST A jolly good company too. In fact, its monopoly is our saving-grace. Why, only last month, I purchased 225 slaves with a jolly good, handsome, return on investment.

PETER BRISTOL Good man!

GUEST Although we did have a negligible loss of 20% of the Negro cargo; with 14 slaves dying in the hold, whilst waiting for our ship to arrive at the African coast. Then, 10 of them deliberately threw themselves overboard on the way here, and a further 21 died from sickness, whilst crossing the Atlantic. But all in all, we secured a handsome price for the sale of the Negroes to the tune of £5560 8s and 5d.

ALL *(Varied responses)*
Bravo!
Capital!
Well done!

GUEST Yes, Captain Ellis Falls did a splendid job comanding the ship.

GUEST I say, old Chap; that really *is* a handsome fortune. Let's all drink to your wealth.

ALL *(All raising their glasses)* Hear! Hear! To your wealth!

PETER BRISTOL I must say I've been lucky to benefit from both trading to and from Africa, to be in control of my slaves arriving here. It means my fingers are firmly held on the pulse: from the starting line in Africa, to arrivals on this plantation. There's perhaps a little more cost involved but having my own captains makes it easier for me to manage. The real challenge, of course, is the scarcity of sugar on the return to Britain; that's why we need more slaves. We were lucky to purchase the other day some brass dishes, iron pots, Manchester cloth, beads, copper rods, pipes and tobacco, among other things, to sail the *Africa Queen,* in exchange for more slaves in Africa.

GUEST I agree, we need more Negroes to work here. They are the sinews of a plantation and it's impossible for a man to make sugar without them.

GUEST Well, since my arrival, I have purchased 20 Negro slaves and I must say, I was shocked and repulsed at the same time, at the sight of naked human flesh exposed in the way that it was, for sale. However, I can only say that my investment has brought me real dividends.

PETER BRISTOL Come, come man, *repulsed? (Laughing)* Repulsion is for the weak. Surely you must be convinced that God ordained the Negroes for our use, and to benefit us: otherwise the Divine would probably manifest other thinking, in some other way *(He shrugs)*; surely not in the way that it is now.

LADY GUEST Yes, if not, the Good Lord would have willed it otherwise, surely?

MRS. BRISTOL Why, even the Good Book says that, *"slaves must obey their masters."* This is a clear indication that these Negroes were given to us, for our work and pleasure.

GUEST Well, let's just say it is impossible for a man to make sugar without Negroes; that's why I bought a sugar-mill and extra land to be cultivated, so I bought 9 extra slaves.

PETER BRISTOL Gentlemen, learn from my strategy. You must buy the minimum number of slaves, work them hard; maybe hire extra when you need them. Remember, the death rate among them is high; a beastly expense to us.

GUEST I've managed by keeping and feeding my Negroes enough, and encourage them to grow their own provisions. Economic sense really; they can grow their own provisions, without you having to spend money to feed them. That way, you get more work from them; they continue to be healthy and so on.

GUEST You have a point there, avoid expenses like calling for a doctor to Negroes, as much as possible. And the fact remains, these doctors are too damned expensive. Slaves' growing their own food is a healthy option - less sick Negroes. So keep away from giving favours, like doctors; it could become a rod for your own back and the lazy scums would feign sickness, at an alarming rate!

GUEST And on this subject of generosity, I would say don't grant *particular* favours and take care not to do so frequently. I mean, giving them a day off like Sunday; our Lord's day, but not with regularity, as it would encourage idleness and laziness, neglect of work; even labouring in their own plots of ground for their own food.

GUEST Well, what I have to say is this, the Slave trade is the best God-given favour a man could ever want. There's enough in the chain of workers to make profits to fund more slave ships. We pay small businessmen and craftsmen to supply our goods for exchange. There are enough dock-workers to unload the cargoes of sugar, rum and tobacco. We pay for their daily work and of course, not forgetting the African enablers in Africa, who capture the slaves and keep them on hold for us, at the coast.

PETER BRISTOL *(Flushed pink and animated)* Gentlemen, long may our slavery fortunes last! We fund new ships, spread some wealth at home, through charitable works and not forgetting to donate to our churches – so, *everyone* gains from our trade.

GUEST *(Animatedly)* Doesn't that make us Captains of the Slave Trade industry? Who knows, it may yet fuel an industrial revolution in Britain!

PETER BRISTOL A splendid projection indeed; then, long may the Slave Triangle last!

ALL *(Guffaws and eating heartily).* Ha! Ha! Long may it last! Indeed!

[Curtain closes

ANANCY You know, there's an old proverb which goes like this *"Teeth don't always laugh good things."* See how they're laughing? What's funny or good about stealing people, exchanging them for goods and brutally selling and re-selling them? Then turning them into slaves, to work on Plantations thousands of miles away from their homes and *never* seeing their loved ones again? *(She pauses):*
Eh, tell me, what's funny about that? Well, I leave you to ponder an answer for this one.
  (Anancy sings as she leaves the stage)

"Everyman has a right to his freedom!"

[Exeunt

ACT 4 SCENE 2 - THE CANE WORK-SONG

SETTING: *Very early morning 5 am on the Plantation. Slaves (men, women and children) are greeting Gang-Gang Sarah, as they pass her cabin, on their way to the cane field. They are jubilant, as they anticipate receiving their monthly sack of cornmeal after work; which Gang-Gang Sarah is tasked with distributing.*

STAGE DIRECTIONS: *Light blue stage lighting scene is outside, shown as a silhouette with trees in the background.*

GANG-GANG *(Stands at the front of her cabin talking to workmen and women as they pass her. They are heading towards the cane-field).* Marnin', howdy-doo, one and all.

SEPTIMUS Howdy-do madam, you aright?

GANG-GANG Yes ah dey, jus' fighting the devils, in every way, you know, as usual. You comin' to get your sack of corn later? Remind the others to come early eh. I have a lot of work to do and still plenty people linin' up for help.

SEPTIMUS We know, we know, and believe me, when ah say we *really* appreciate you.

GANG-GANG Well thanks, eh! Because Janet may give birth tonight, she in labour for so long, I have to be there; A few sick people to visit and give medicine; making bush medicine is not a one minute job. After that, we have *Kumina* ritual tonight again, behind the fields. We have to do *Ogun* for a few people; if not, disaster will strike this Plantation!

SEPTIMUS A'right, a'right, ah hear you. Doh worry, eh, I'll make sure and tell everybody. We'll come early, so we won't hold you up. We go see later, then.

GANG-GANG Okay, thanks eh, and walk good.

YOUNG ANA *(Greets Gang-Gang Sarah as she passes by on her way to the cane field)* Mornin' Ma!

GANG-GANG Chile, marnin.' May *Ogun* fight for you today, and protect you. My spiritual eye showin' me what they plannin' for you, behind your back.

    (She shivers then shakes her head in disgust)
    Just walk good chile. You need to come an' see me urgently tonight, for a protection to wear, eh?
YOUNG ANA Yes Antie, I will come tonight, Antie!
GANG-GANG *(Mutters under her breath)*
    Too much abusin' of our young girls; look at her! Imagine, to be raped at the age of 10! In 9 month's time she'll be carrying white Massah child inside her, which he will eventually sell, because half-breeds with near-white skin fetch more money on slave markets.
    (She shakes her head)
    Noh, noh, noh! Too much! *Ogun*, please watch over her today! *(She goes back into her cabin)*

ON THE CANE FIELD: *(Everyone is cutting cane on the plantation. They take it in turn to sing this Call- and-Response work-song, as they cut the cane).*

THE SUGAR CANE WORK-SONG

LEADER	Oh dem ol' pretty bitter-sweet cane, Fine cane, long cane, cane is pain,
WORKERS	*But love 'em hate 'em, all the same,* *Cane not mine; cane pain not for me.*
LEADER	Fine cane, long cane, cane is pain, Jus' cut de cane, Jus' cut the cane,
WORKERS	*Follow me; I follow you, cutting cane,* *Cane not mine; cane pain not for me.*
LEADER	See dat pretty gal cutting right there, She will cook nice corn jus' for you,
WORKERS	*Cut the cane quick; jus' follow me,.* *Cane not mine; cane pain not for me.*
LEADER	Her plate of corn will be big tonight, It make you big, you will feel a'right,
WORKERS	*Fine cane, long cane, cane is pain,* *Cane not mine; cane pain not for me.*

LEADER	Smell it, taste it, smell dat nice corn,
	Roast it, shell it, we'll boil it real soon,
WORKERS	*Fine cane, long cane, cane is pain,*
	Cane not mine; cane pain not for me.

[Exeunt

ACT 4 SCENE 3 - CHRISTIANISING ADE

SETTING: *In the Verandah of the Great House, sitting comfortably on lounging chairs. Mrs. Bristol and her two children (Peter Jr and Stella, 12 yr old twins) are relaxing, and sheltering from the extreme heat. Mrs. Bristol is reading from the Bible to the children, to pass the time away. They are attended by Ade, an African Muslim house-slave.*
STAGE DIRECTIONS: *17 year old Ade is standing over the family with a portable fan; slowly fanning them from the day's intense heat. He tries to show disinterest in their activity, though he is fascinated by their "Talking Book."*

MRS BRISTOL *(Flustered and irritated, she complains to her Children, as she mops her brow).* This infernal heat is hellish, only the Good Lord can give us protection from it. Come you two, it's time for today's story; let's hear what the *Good Book* has to say.

STELLA *(Excited and moving closer to her mother)* Which story is it today, mother?

MRS BRISTOL I think the story of Moses and Pharaoh is as good as any, I s'pose.
(She reads from her Bible, then paraphrases her explanations to the children)
"Not only did Pharaoh refuse to let the Israelites go, but from then on, he made their work even harder! He said that the slaves would have to keep making the same number of bricks, but they wouldn't be provided with the straw they needed. That meant they would have to go gather their own straw before they could make their bricks. Now the work would take even longer!"

PETER Jr *(Irritated by the heat he snaps at Ade)* Faster Ade, fan us faster, and stop listening to **our** story. It's not for you, and besides, you're a slave and slaves can't be Christians. Isn't that right mother?

ADE *(Aside)* Can't be a *Christian*? Me, Ade? Huh! They think ah don't undersand everythin' they say! Well, I'm a Muslim boy. I love and understand my own book, the *Koran*. I'm not stupid! S-t-u-p-e-s! Keep your damn Christian paranoia and fears to yourself!

MRS BRISTOL Mmm! I don't know, sometimes I think perhaps it's better these Negroes should be given some sort of moral education about what the *Good Book* says, but I also understand that it would be dangerous to teach them to read.

STELLA But they *can't* read, mother! And who would teach them?

MRS BRISTOL It's strictly forbidden to teach them. On one hand, they could probably be *Followers* of the Word but definitely not *Christians;* no not like us. In fact, enlightening them might just make them defy their positions as slaves, and then where would we be? Best to keep the slaves where they belong.

PETER Jr Father says I can have my own slaves when I grow up. Will I have this Plantation too, mother?

MRS. BRISTOL By all accounts, I believe it will be passed on to you some day, in the future. *(Taking him by the shoulder so that he faces her directly).* That's why even now, you must listen, look and learn all there is to know about controlling and managing the Negroes. They're a very complicated lot!

STELLA As for me, I think I'ill be going home to England some day. I'll take my fortunes and live in London. Plus, it's far too hot here in the Caribbean and I can't wait to make friends.

MRS. BRISTOL *(She sighs loudly and closes the Bible)*
All in good time, my dears, all in good time.

STELLA *(Excitedly)* Do tell us about back home in England, mother. Sometimes, I just want to sit and dream about my future there.

PETER Jr And I'd like to hear about the churches in England my father belonged to and the kind of charity he used to give to them when you were there.

MRS BRISTOL Well Peter, I think that your father would be best to tell you about that. But as for telling you about England, *(she becomes animated)*, there's so much to tell, and just where do I start? *(She motions to Peter to sit next to her)*

BOTH CHILDREN *(Both children move closer to her)* Anywhere!

MRS. BRISTOL Well, we come from the city of Bristol, just like our surname; now there's a coincidence, if ever I knew one. Our house, quite a fair size, had a lovely garden, with a small water fountain, beautifully trimmed hedges and all the windows had plenty of glass; not like others, we invested in the latest materials. Inside, there was the Great Hall, and the walls were covered with tapestries and oak panelling to keep out the drafts.

STELLA Mother, what's a draught?

MRS. BRISTOL Well, in the winter time, when it's bitterly cold, the rooms have to be heated and if the freezing cold wind secretly blows up from, say underneath the door frame, the burst of wind that sneaks from outside feels very cold; we call it a draught.

PETER Jr Must have been beastly cold then? *(He sighs loudly)* Too cold there, too hot here!

MRS. BRISTOL *(Nodding her head in agreement)*
Anyway, one thing in common with being here, was our 4 poster bed. But we had curtains all around and tapestries hung on the walls, as decorations. Of course, you could say we had some wealth, because our plates, dishes, bowls, as well as spoons, were made of silver and pewter and few items in gold. And everything was taken care of by Lizzie, our servant; who cured bacon and salted our meat to preserve it. And sugar was so scarce; we used honey to sweeten things. Anyway, enough of that for today. Run along now, it's almost supper time.

[Exit Children

MRS. BRISTOL *(Contemplative, she shakes her head)*
Oh, how I *miss* those times at home, back in England!
ANANCY *(Enters)* And *me*, how I *miss* my home in Africa. And as for the slaves, how they *miss* their homes in Africa too! The only difference is, we don't stand a chance in hell, of ever going back, or seeing our loved ones again. I Anancy, and the rest of my brethren from the African Continent, are destined to die right here. So, If old age and sickness don't kill us, believe me when I say, this back-breaking, big, heavy, donkey-work, definitely will! Yeah man, this Caribbean is our last stop!

(Anancy sings as she exits): "Go down Moses, way down in Egypt land, tell old Pharoah, let my people go!"

[Exit Anancy

ACT 4 SCENE 4 - PASS IT ON! - *THE KALINDA*

STAGE DIRECTION: *Blue stage lighting scene at the end of the day's work, Ade returned to his slave compound with many questions in his mind. He passes on his experience to the group of slaves, who are relaxing and exchanging experiences, after a long day's work. There's drumming from the gathered group.*

SETTING: *A group of slaves are seated on the ground in a circle. They are exchanging stories about their experiences of the day by dancing the scenarios in the centre of the ring. This style of passing on information, in song, is via the call-and-response oral transmission in the Caribbean. The group begin their evening reverie with the Kalinda, a combative dance of stick fighting, with 2 men in the ring; the others are seated, singing and drumming.*

TWO MEN   From the day a hold me bois,
Me mudder call me a murderer,
Mama, mama, doh cry for me,
Me, bois man, no fraid nobody!
Bois!

TWO MEN   Ah playing anybody they put in the ring.
But me, bois man, no 'fraid nobody!
No bois man no 'fraid nobody,
No bois man no 'fraid nobody,
Me, bois man, no 'fraid no demon!
Bois!

TWO MEN   Mooma, you son in the grave already,
Take a towel and band your belly,
No, bois man no 'fraid no body,
No, bois man no 'fraid no body.
Bois!
(Playful teasing from the women who enter the ring)

TWO WOMEN   Tire mama, tire mama!
Tire mama, tire mama!
No woman no 'fraid no bois man,
Any woman could beat a bois man!

                  Any woman could beat a bois man!
                  Bois!
                  (There's much laughter, singing and dancing; then Ade takes the centre stage)

ADE CALLS   Today I hear a Bible story 'bout how Moses fight:
                  Pass it on, ah say *pass it on!*

GROUP RESPONSE   A man call Moses, he say, *pass it on.*

ADE CALLS   'Gainst Pharoah, a cruel man-king:
                  pass It on, ah say *pass it on!*

GROUP RESPONSE   A Pharoah king he say, *pass it on.*

ADE CALLS   Let my people go, Moses say to king:
                  pass it on, ah say *pass it on!*

GROUP RESPONSE   Let people go, he say, *pass it on.*

ADE CALLS   So we mus' tell our Massah to let us go:
                  pass it on, ah say *pass it on.*

GROUP RESPONSE   Massah mus' let us go; he say, *pass it on.*

ADE CALLS   If he don't, we make him let us go:
                  We make Massah let us go, ah say *pass it on!*

GROUP RESPONSE   Make Massah let us go, he say *pass it on.*

ADE CALLS   "*Talking book*" say He'll wipe up our tears:
                  Pass it on, ah say *pass it on!*

GROUP RESPONSE   He'll wipe our tears, he say *pass it on.*

ADE CALLS   It's not for me alone, it's for everyone:
                  Pass it on, ah say *pass it on!*

GROUP RESPONSE   It's for all of us, he say *pass it on.*
                  (3 other men join Ade in the centre stage, as he dances. Drumming, then individuals shout from the group as the dancing and singing rise to a crescendo).
                  "One!" *(1ˢᵗ Man jumps in the ring dancing the Kalinda vibrantly, shouts)*
                  "Tell Massah to let us go!"
                  (Group responds while others join in the dance)

GROUP Let us go! We say let us go!
(Drumming, then another person shouts from the group)
"**Two**!" *(2nd Man jumps in the ring dancing the Kalinda vibrantly, shouts)*
Trouble, go dey, if he say no.
(Group responds as others join in the dance)

GROUP Let us go! We say let us go!
(Drumming, then a 3rd person shouts from the group)
"**Three**!" *(3rd Man jumps in the ring dancing the Kalinda Vibrantly shouts)* –
With fire, an' cutlass, we will fight.
(Group response as others joins in the Kalinda dance)

GROUP Let us go! We say we will fight!
(All three men *CALL*)

THREE MEN Massah, Massah; we say, let us go!
(Group RESPONSE)

GROUP Let us go, we say let us go!
(Repeat)
(All three men *CALL*)

THREE MEN Massah, Massah; we say let us go.
(Group RESPONSE)

GROUP We will fight, we say let us go!
(Drumming, slaves' voices & lighting fade slowly)

[Exeunt

ANANCY And so it is, the seeds of discontent simmers and festers, like open sores that just won't cure but continue to grow in size and contagion. Young Ade understood the imilarity between what he had heard in the Bible story of the Israelites in Egypt, and the slaves' own situation here in the Caribbean. Yes, that Exodus story added flames to their repressed fire, which re-ignited, they passed on. So the prevailing emotions of anger, incessant pain and suffering, repetitive frustrations, deep-seated resentment, suppressed emotions; amid calls for things to change, are festering too. Rumours are rife on plantations here; some are more active on plantations nearby; of secret rebellions being plotted and estates they will burn down. Of Plantation owners who would suddenly fall sick of illness that no white man medicine will cure. The desire for freedom is a hurricane force, that will errupt like a festering volcano. Plans are afoot, so be warned! Sssshhhh!

[Exits

ACT 4 SCENE 5 – OBEAH MAN & THE SILK COTTON TREE

SETTING: *In the woods near to a silk cotton tree. Stanjosef, an Obeah man, is consulted by clients for assistance in the African magical arts. Slaves on the Plantation are afraid for their lives, as Mr. Bristol, the Plantation Owner, has given them orders to clear some land with a silk cotton tree on it; in order to extend his canefield. The feared, but revered silk cotton tree, stands in the selected path, and slaves are very fearful of the consequences of cutting down this special tree; which has links with evil spirits and ancestors.*

STAGE DIRECTION: *Floodlit blue stage lighting, with black silhouetted trees, night sounds; (crickets and fireflies). Inside a cabin in the woods is Mr. Stanjosef, speaking to his obeah clients. They are two Cane-cutters, who are refusing to cut down a silk cotton tree as ordered, and are very afraid of the consequences on either side: spiritual repercussions for interfering with the silk cotton tree or getting a whipping to death, from the Slave managers, for refusing to obey an order to cut the tree.*

(Stealthily two Cane-cutters enter Stanjosef's little hut in the woods)

1ˢᵗ CANE-CUTTER Baba, ah fraid for me life, oh! Massah, he say cut down dat silk cotton tree; make room to plant more cane. But is 'fraid, ah'fraid, oh. Cyan cut down no jumbie tree! What ah go do, sah?

STANJOSEF *(Rising up from his seat angrilly)*
What! No mad white man go cut down dat silk cotton tree! Or its enemy must die. Dat tree is the home of hundreds of spirits! You see all those nails ah drive into dat tree trunk; each one is a spirit of a dead person dat I and others call, to leave a person's body an' come there. For years I been chasin' bad spirits, healin' people right there and makin' medicine from dat same old tree.

1ˢᵗ CANE-CUTTER I know Baba, only last year, littl' boy David was cleared of dysentery with medicine from de same tree, and I hear women with bleedin' sickness and sex disease get cured from dat tree medicine too.

2nd CANE-CUTTER Well yes, dey say Ol' Joe pass out two littl' stones, all de way from his kidneys, by drinkin' medicine made from de tree; leaves, bark and flowers – everythin'. So is 'fraid, I 'fraid oh! 'Cause I no go cut down no tree, Baba!

STANJOSEF Look around you. It's the biggest tree you can see for miles and miles - no one *ever* dares to disturb *Damballah*, the great Snake God: for a hundred years and more, he been livin' in dat tree!

1st CANE-CUTER An' *Papa Bois,* the Father of the forest – he'll cause great disaster for dat Massah too, for touchin' his forest. Is not so, sah? Please oh, you mus' do *somethin'* to help, or he'll kill us if we refuse to cut down the tree, in three days' time.

STANJOSEF Eh heh! Don't he know dat disturbin' our ancestors in dis rude way, has many terrible consequences? Even death! Yes, horrible death! We mus' call for a guardian spirit to stand guard for dis tree. There mus' be an urgent exchange of life, to save dat silk cotton tree; startin' from tonight.

CANE-CUTTERS Dat is very good sah! Make it quick-quick, before 3 days time, please sah. Is 'fraid, ah 'fraid oh!

STANJOSEF Gimme your Massah name. An' while you're at it, gimme names of his family too. Pass me those nails on the table there!

1st CANE-CUTTER He has twin children sah, a boy an' a girl!

STANJOSEF
Twins! Twin sex - dats even better still! We'll have two spirits to guard this tree instead of one. They mus' be nailed to dat tree tonight, before he make a single move to cut dat tree down!

CANE-CUTTERS Yes sah! Hurry! Hurry! sah! I think Massah is 'fraid of the tree too; worried 'bout all the people comin' here to visit you, Baba. He say dey not workin' hard enough, if dey wastin' time to come here!

STANJOSEF OK, you mus' go now! I've urgent work to do tonight. Go straight home, quickly, and whatever you do, don't look back until you get inside your cabin.

[Exeunt

ANANCY *(Shaking his head and wagging his spider arm)*
All-you remember what ah said before? There is a stirring in the blood; trouble coming, here and there. I could feel it in the air. Nobody must mess with Papa Bois, the Father of the Forest. He's the Guardian and Keeper of everything in the forest; protector of the animals and defender of land. He 'aint making no joke! The Obeah man too, he aint making no joke! Basil the Devil, who also live inside that Silk Cotton tree, he aint making no joke either!
So Anancy saying it's not *black* magic, it's medicine magic; for all sorts of cures – medicine for sickness and medicine for evil men too! And even I, Anancy, aint making no joke! Massah better watch out, trouble coming deh! Yes, trouble coming for sure!
(She shakes her head)
All-you better watch out too, eh! Silk cotton tree deh for hundreds of years, 200 hundred feet tall, tough like hell. Dey say, sometimes at night, these trees move about an' gather together, to consult one another. All-you, doh joke with our silk cotton tree, eh! Ssshhh!!

[Exits

ACT 4 SCENE 6 – KARMIC EFFECT IN THE GREAT HOUSE

SETTING: *At Peter Bristol's home, where the twins have become gravely ill. Mrs. Bristol is beside herself with grief. The doctor is sent for but he's mystified by their illness and is unable to cure them. They worsen during the night and in desperation a house slave suggests enlisting the help of Gang-Gang Sarah and her African medicine. Mrs Bristol agrees, defying her husband's vehement disapproval.*

STAGE DIRECTION: *The stage is flood-lit with red lighting; showing a bedroom scene with the two Bristol children lying unconscious. It is the middle of the night. Mrs. Bristol kneels beside them crying and mumbling incoherent words. Two senior house-slaves are in attendance - the female house-slave, with hand basin and cloth, is mopping the twins' brows; while the male house-slave increases the lighting in the house.*

MRS BRISTOL *(Crying unconrollably she pleads with her husband)* I beg you Pete, do something now, quickly! They are barely breathing, Peter. Get help for my babies! Get help, please! I beg you!

PETER BRISTOL *(Consoling his wife)* OK my dear, I know, I understand but it's important not to panic, dear. We'll go and fetch Dr Evans right away. *(He pats her reassuringly on the shoulder)* He just needs to be here, I'm sure he will be able to sort this situation out. So, stop worrying so much.
(He calls to the male house slave) Go fetch my horse immediately! And come, ride with me to Dr. Evans. *(Walking towards the door impatiently, he shouts)* Get moving now, man!

MRS BRISTOL *(To the female house slave)*
Let's try some smelling salts. There is a small brown bottle in a box, on my dressing table; fetch it immediately; we must help them to breathe. We must keep them awake.

HOUSE SLAVE *(Curtseying)* Yes Ma'am, I bring it right away, Ma'am.

MRS BRISTOL *(Desparing, she speaks to her sick semi-conscious children)*
Stay awake darlings, you must both stay awake. The doctor will be here soon. I promise you, it will be alright when he comes. O God, please make it alright! You'll see, he's coming soon; just stay awake, darlings, please - I beg you to stay awake! *(She cries uncontrollably)*

HOUSE SLAVE *(Returning to the room)*
Here, Ma'am, I have the little brown bottle. What to do with it, Ma'am?

MRS BRISTOL Give it to me!
(She puts the smelling salt bottle to each child's nose; there's only a weak cough response, but nothing more. There is movement outside in the yard. Mr. Bristol has returned with Dr. Evans, who promptly makes his way to the children)

PETER BRISTOL Well, my dear, any improvements?

MRS BRISTOL No, Pete, they're worse, *(she cries)* Pete, they're getting worse by the hour!

PETER BRISTOL OK, no more panicking, the doctor's here now so, let him do his work. I'll be in the Drawing Room.

DR EVANS *(Examining each child, he seems very concerned about their pulses)*
And how long would you say they have been lying here like this?

MRS. BRISTOL Since 6 o'clock this evening, doctor.

DR EVANS Have they drunk or eaten anything unusual today? Any complaints of chest pains, or pains anywhere else in their bodies?

MRS BRISTOL Why, no doctor, none whatsoever! They were

perfectly in good spirits all day but around 6pm, after supper, Peter Junior complained of headaches and generally feeling unwell and within one hour, Stella also complained of the same unwell feelings too!
We put them to bed immediately and they just went from bad to worse; now this. *(She points to the two helpless children)* Please doctor, help them? There must be something you can do!

DR EVANS *(Frowning and puzzled)*
This case just seems uniquely unexplainable!
(He scratches his head, and touches his beard)
Some blood tests would be the next best action, of course, but it's the middle of the night; so that's out of the question right now. *(Turning to the House slave)*
We need to undress them. Assist me quickly; let's check for possible unusual insect bite marks.
(Tone of disappointment with no visible marks)
I must say, this situation is highly irregular, yes, most strange; I haven't seen anything like this before! Both of them with the same condition, at the same time!
(He closes his doctor's kit and leaves the bedroom, in search of Peter Bristol in the Drawing Room)

PETER BRISTOL *(Standing next to a sideboard with a decanter with brandy and a glass half-full in his hand, his back towards the doctor)*
Well, how are they now, Doc? I expect you were able to get to the root of this small problem, yes?
(He takes a swig at his brandy and drinks it in one gulp: pours another one and continues to speak, without turning around to look at Dr. Evans)
You know, *(His back still towards Dr. Evans, he pours another brandy),* I told my wife, don't you worry dear; *(He gulps down the drink in one go).*
Just leave it to the good old doctor, he takes care of everything! He'll know what to do with our babies!

(Then, Peter Bristol turns to face the doctor, staring straight into his eyes, for solace)

DR EVANS Look, I'm so sorry, old chap; I couldn't live up to your high expectations tonight. There seems to be more than meet the eye here. I did the usual examination but I'm at a loss to figure out what is happening here; and with both children! I must say I've not come across anything like this before! I can't give them any medicine as they are in a semi-conscious state. I've tried my best to make them comfortable. Now, let's just see what happens in the morning, eh.
(He reassuringly pats Peter Bristol on his shoulder, as he leaves)
I will be back early tomorrow, with more amunition, as we say. So chin up, old boy!

[Exit Dr. Evans

MRS BRISTOL *(Moves to the Drawing Room, distraught, crying, pleading helplessly to her husband)*
Pete, doctor said he can't help us! *You* said he would be able to help us but he *can't* and my babies are lying there, as if they're ***dead!*** *(Wails uncontrollably)*

PETER BRISTOL *(Speaking angrily but with bravado)*
Now, pull yourself together woman! And don't ever use *that* word in this house again!

MRS BRISTOL *(Raising her voice)* Alright then, I won't say it for now but Edith, over there, senior house Slave, says she knows someone who can help us with this type of sickness. You know which one, that Birth Attendant on the Estate. Edith says she has delivered hundreds of babies on this Plantation right here for us. *(Anxiously, she grabs him by the arm)* I tell you, this Gang-Gang person, who is helping all the slaves, maybe she can help cure our children. You need to fetch her now, Pete! Since it is the only chance we have right now!

(She drops to her knees, holding onto his leg, crying uncontrollably)

PETER BRISTOL *(Sternly)* Don't be stupid woman! Have you taken leave of your senses too? *(Half laughing)* Who's ever heard of a *slave* being able to do what a fully qualified Englishman; a trained medical doctor, can't do?
(He laughs whilst still drinking more brandy, then raises his voice)
I think you're damn mad to put *our* children's lives in the hands of a *slave!* And besides, where's your faith in God?
(He drinks a lot more brandy and noisily puts the glass down)

MRS BRISTOL *(Wailing)* But tomorrow may be too late, Pete!!

PETER BRISTOL OK, since you seem to have completely lost your mind and perhaps I won't hear the last of it, should anything go wrong; do what you want to! Send for your bloody bush doctor! Now, get out of my sight!

(Now intoxicated, he becomes delirious, laughing and crying helplessly, at the same time).

[Exeunt

ACT 4 SCENE 7 - MORAL AND SPIRITUAL DILEMMAS

SETTING: *It's the dead of night and everyone is asleep. Gang-Gang is secretly visited at her slave cabin and is asked to accompany two house slaves, Edith and Ade, to the Bristol's Great House. Gang-Gang Sarah is fast asleep; dreaming. She is visited by Gamab the god of life, and Gaunab, the god of evil and death, as well as Papa Legba; with a message from the Supreme God Olodurame, who suggests the right course of action that Gang-Gang should take.*

STAGE DIRECTION: *Gang-Gang is in her cabin, lying on a bed, in a corner. Voices are amplified sounds, coming from outside of Gang-Gang's cabin. There's loud knocking on Gang-Gang's door. She jumps up from her bed, looking for her shawl and head-wrap. Grabbing the shawl, she ties her head as she goes to the door.*

GANG-GANG *(Persistent loud knocking)* Hold on! Hold on! I'm coming! I'm coming, *Oya*, give me strength! Is this day never going to end?

EDITH *(Out of breath and anxious)*
Ma-ma, you mus' come quick! Massah children, dey dying, bring medicine now!

GANG-GANG *(Looking puzzled and surprised)*

Wha' you saying? Hold on! The white people want *me* to go into their Great House and give black medicine to *their* children? Whoever hear of this? Is it a trick of the white devil?

EDITH No ma! Not a trick! But you mus' come quick or dey dead, oh!

GANG-GANG *(Agitated)* You sure you did see sick children?

ADE Yes, de white doctor, he come for Massah children, he Cyan help dem. He say, if dey alive in the marnin,' he go come back but he don' know what to do. So you mus' come quick! De Madam cryin' mightily. Her babies lay on bed like dead dummies. Duppy got their soul for sure, but I know you can help dem to come back, Ma!

GANG-GANG Eh! Eh! *(Scowling disdainfully)* Oh, so they need *my* help now, yes? The great, powerful, white Massah

              need help from me, Gang-Gang, you did say so, eh?
ADE   Yes Ma, but you have to hurry, come quick, oh!
GANG GANG *(Angrily)* Eh-eh! so the white children life matter more than the black slave babies that they beat each and every day, on their plantation estate! As you know, every single day, eight year old babies are working alongside men and women, doing 12-hour shifts in cane fields. And with just one meal a day! They're whipped just like any one of us, to cut cane in the hot sun! As soon as they reach 10 years, some even before 10 years, they are raped; some killed! And these same people want *my* help for *their* precious children!
ADE   Yes ma! Ah know, Ah know, ma, but….!
GANG GANG *(Angrily & loudly interrupting)*
              But, who does comes to save slave children? Who comes to protect them? Who gives them white medicine when they sick? Don't Massah have plenty money? Does he buy food for slave children, eh?
ADE   No ma! But…
GANG GANG No buts, he can buy his own medicine or bury his own two children! And that's that! Go back and tell them I'm *not* coming to save *anybody*!
              (Angrily, Gang Gang slams the door in the Slaves' faces and refuses to go outside. A little while later, there is gentle knocking on her door)
GANG GANG *(She's talking to herself before she opens the door, thinking the house slaves had knocked again)*
              I said, the children will have to die because me, I'm *not* coming out to go to no white massah Great House!
              (Opening the front door, there's no one there. She's puzzled, so closes the door again – minutes later, there is a gentle knock, again)

GANG GANG *(Opens the door again, to find there's still no one there)* Is my tired mind playing tricks on me, at this god-forsaken hour of the night! Even all cock-fowl, donkey, goat and pig can sleep in peace.
(Pushing her head out slowly, she looks up and down, cautiously).
Is who there? And don't bother playing tricks, it's too late in the night for all this game-playing. Show yourself!
(There is no one there, but a voice can be heard outside)

VOICE OF GAMAB It is I, Gamab, the supreme diety, god of life and death, from the sky. I direct the fate of mankind and decide their time of death. Pay heed to my message - it is not yet time for the white children's death, my daughter. You must put aside your anger, pain and revenge; since it is not in your hands to decide who lives and die.

GANG-GANG *(Falls on her knees in fear)*
Eh! Oh sah, Sarry Oh! Sarry, sah!

VOICE OF GAMAB Do you decide who feeds the birds of the air and the fish of the sea?

GANG-GANG *(Shakes her head profusely and fearfully)*
No! No! Sah, me, Gang-Gang don't!

VOICE OF GAMAB Well then, do what you must! And do it now!
(Voice fades. Closing the front door, and gathering things to put into her bag of medicine, there's another knock on her door)

GANG GANG *(Talking loudly to herself)*
Now, it's past the dead of night, and I think everyone must have decided, 'oh that Gang-Gang, she must not sleep tonight.' Even the gates of hell has less visitors in one night!
(Confrontationally, she goes to open the door but there's still no one there)
Hello! Hello! Is this some kind of knock-knock-who's-there game? I ask again, who's there? Show yourself or get lost!

VOICE OF GAUNAB *(An angry, loud, thunderous rasping voice)*
> It is I, Gaunab, god of death, misfortune and sickness. Did not the Obeah man call on me yesterday, at the silk cotton tree, and gifted me with two young souls?
> *(Laughs a wicked cackle)*
> Yes, as the arch enemy of your first visitor, I dare you to go to that Great House! Matters to resolve the dispute with the silk cotton tree has already been taken care of. The white devil *must* reap the consequence of all his actions and words. You just heard from Gamab, my arch enemy, who told you to go. He is a damn soft fool – always preaching non-violence, whilst people continue to die as helpless victims. Their peaceful approach makes them so stupid they will even lay their heads down on a chopping block; for what? Idiots! To please the white devil! No!!
> *(Loudly & angrily)* Because I, Gaunab, say *No! We must fight back!*

GANG-GANG You mean the god of life and the god of death are both at war, over the sick children of the white man, sah?

GAUNAB No! I wouldn't say *war*. I call it revenge, retribution, pay-back time!
> *(His laugh is a cackle)*
>
> But there will be war in the white man's yard alright; fire in his field; angry mobs in his estate; the price of revenge has already been paid for, in full. Trouble is brewing! The fate of the white man has been sealed. You, Gang-Gang, whose name means *"one who will lead,"* if you stand in the way, you too will pay for interferring. Go back to your bed! Gaunab, the god of disease, death and misfortune speaks! By morning the children will die.
>
> *(He laughs a very loud wild cackle which fades; she closes the door).*

GANG-GANG *(Shaking her head in disbelief)*
Well, that's it! If I was ever thinking of having a peaceful night's sleep, I'm very mistaken. First, one set of instructions, then another set of instructions! Do this! Don't do this! Save them, let them die! Can anything else make my night more nightmarish? Where do I stand? *(Contemplating quietly)* I'm between a war of spiritual conflict; caught in the middle of good and evil forces vying for dominance. Me, little me, slave, warrior, medicine, woman; sandwich between them over here, and with dying children over there. *(Stretching out her palms alternately)* Shall I? Shall I not?
(Another knock on Gang-Gang's door, she goes to open)
For the love of …..
(Shocked at the visitor standing at her door).
Oh, Papa! Did they send you too? Is the white massah children dead?

PAPA LEGBA I'm Legba, god of the crossroads and humble messenger from the most powerful and wise one. As god of the crossroads, where the children's souls are now waiting, I am tasked to travel miles, over the sea and over the heavens, with one message for you, my daughter. This message is from Olorun or Olodumare, as you always call him;the most Supreme God. He says, these same children will, one day, be responsible for making changes to *our* people's future lives for the better. Therefore, their end-time on earth is not now. You must go and save the children!

GANG-GANG *(She falls on her knees in astonishment)* Is this from Olodumare himself, Papa?

PAPA LEGBA Yes, from the master himself. The most powerful and wise god has sent me, with one simple order. *'Gang-Gang must go and save the white children's lives, as she has done to countless other children, all her life.'*
Olodumare is very pleased with you, my daughter, and has

much joy and happiness in store for you. Go my child - go to the big house and save the white man's children now; for your time of reward is nigh!
(He disappears. Gang-Gang Sarah is fast asleep, tossing and turning. There's loud knocking on her door. She jumps up from her dream, looking for her shawl and head-wrap. Grabbing the shawl, she ties her head, as she heads towards the door).

GANG-GANG *(Persistent loud knocking)* Hold on! Hold on! I'm coming, Oya, give me strength! Is this day never going to end?

EDITH *(Out of breath and anxious)* Mam, you mus' come quick! Massah children, dey dying, bring medicine now!

GANG-GANG *(Looking very puzzled)* Eh! wha' you saying, hold on! The *white* people want me to go into *their* house now, and give *black* medicine to their sick *white* children? Haaaaa!
(Shaking her head in disbelief, she appears a little confused, as her dream flashes back to her)
So, w-w-wait a minute! I swear I was having the strangest dream about all this: the children, and some visitors - many visitors, and you and.....!

EDITH *(Interrupting impatiently)* Hurry, Mam, Hurry, we have transport to take you there, come quick, hurry, dey dying, oh!

GANG GANG *(Hurriedly grabs her medicine bag)* OK! OK! Hold on, I'm coming!

[Exeunt

Act 5 SCENE 1 - GANG-GANG'S REWARD: *A NAME!*

SETTING: *A Room in the Bristol's Great House. Mr. & Mrs. Bristol are having an after-dinner conversation, whilst relaxing in the Drawing Room. Peter is excited about a new ruling he wants to instigate beginning from the next day.*

ANANCY And so it was that our very special Gang-Gang, in saving the Bristols' children's lives, had made an indelible mark on their parents' lives in more ways than was imagined. The twins were restored to good health and Gang-Gang was hailed a very special person. In fact, she was rewarded by being given a Christian name – *Sarah*. What Gang-Gang Sarah had done, according to the Bristols, was *'the Lord's work;'* which instantly made her the 'favoured' goose that lays the golden egg on the Plantation. Why, you may ask? You could say that Gang-Gang was the source of financial capital that enabled the Bristols' capitalism, which in turn, nurtured their capitalism back home, in England.
And so began the Bristols' other income stream – developing home-grown human capital, for their Caribbean slave population expansion. But hear noh, old people have a proverb that say,
"What sweet in goat mouth, go turn sour in his *bam-bam!"
All-you watch and see, eh!

(Anancy exits singing: "What sweet in goat mouth, go turn sour in his bam-bam!")

                                                                   [Exits

*bam-bam – Creole language for your *"bottom"*

MRS. BRISTOL *(Head down, doing needlework)* You know darling, I dare say, the Good Lord has been *very* good to us. There's talk of rebellion and all sorts, on other Plantations, at the moment. But with the twins back to normal good health and our co-operating slaves, we could say that we are one of the fortunate ones.

Mr. BRISTOL *(Drawing on his pipe, puffing and blowing smoke out)*
Mmm! Not half! I've been having some thoughts along those same lines myself.

MRS. BRISTOL *(Head still down)* Well, we do have good house slaves and there is that Gang-Gang, whatever her name is.......

MR. BRISTOL *(Interrupting)* I've decided as a reward for her unexplainable service to our kids, to give her a Christian name – something like *Sarah*. Sarah was a good woman and she served not only her husband but also God, and very well too.

MRS. BRISTOL You mean giving her a Christian name would be like making her...mm... you know, more to *our* liking: more acceptable, so to speak.

MR. BRISTOL *(Shaking his head in agreement, coughing as he takes out his pipe)* Precisely! We have those who serve us here in the house too; maybe we should discourage their own type of strange worshipping and get them more on *our* side.

MR. BRISTOL Hmmm!

MRS BRISTOL *(Quickly interjecting before he responds)* Not that they would be called Christians by any means, good Lord **no**; but, at least they could **follow** in our footsteps; since they are in our close and private environment.

MR. BRISTOL *(Thoughtfully)* I think I see where you're coming from.

MRS. BRISTOL Yes, I've always wondered whether some sort of Christian morals need to be passed on to the Negroes; after all, they are mostly in our private space, and wouldn't want any more of their dark arts in our home! Certainly, we could consider maybe baptising those in our homes first, like Ade and Edith, as a start.

MR. BRISTOL *(Putting aside his pipe)* Well, if you must know, I've even gone a stage further in my contemplation. Suddenly, a way forward has been opened for us in a most uncanny way and I believe we should grab it with boths hands!

MRS. BRISTOL *(Puts down the needlework enthusiastically and looks at her husband)*
Go on, I'm all ears.

MR. BRISTOL Well, this Gang-Gang, *Sarah's* special skills, we've already recognised. If we were to task her as Plantation Birth Attendant, with her knowledge and skills, she could be 'officially' in charge of delivering slave babies born on this Caribbean Plantation. What I'm trying to say is, in monetary terms, Gang-Gang *Sarah* could be seen as a lucrative source of income for us.

MRS. BRISTOL *(Puzzled expression)* And how would that work out in everyday terms, I mean?

MR.BRISTOL Well, I figured if we were to really encourage inter-breeding among the slaves, this way we could increase our human-stock here, on the Plantation. It would certainly prevent the huge financial loss of having to raid slaves from Africa and transport them across the Atlantic sea to reach us here.

MRS. BRISTOL *(Excited and enthusiastic)* I see, you clever cloggs! You've wasted no time in calculating the cost benefit of Gang-Gang *Sarah's* promotion, to our very lucrative slave business! Bravo, I salute you!

MR. BRISTOL Not just yet darling, we need to put it into practice first. So tomorrow, I have it in mind to set a new rule for the Slave Managers to implement: starting immediately, the rule is that in-house slave breeding, must take place at a very fast rate, in exchange for some small encouraging rewards and incentives.

MRS. BRISTOL *(On her feet and walking towards a side table with a decanter on it).* Darling, I'd say this is a *wonderful* addition to our income stream!

MR. BRISTOL Yes. It would be firstly, developing home-grown human capital, and secondly, expanding our Caribbean slave fortunes here.

MRS. BRISTOL *(Animatedly)* Splendid idea, really! That calls for a celebratory drink. Brandy, darling?

MR. BRISTOL *(With a self-satisfied smile)* Well, I must say, I don't mind if I do!

[Exeunt

ACT 5 SCENE 2 - APPEASING PAPA BOIS

STAGE DIRECTION: *Blue flood lit stage showing trees in a silhouette background. The Plantation slaves join a small group one by one. They carry items as they prepare to appease Papa Bois, the Guardian of the forest, before cutting down trees to build a cabin.*

SETTING: *Cocks crowing, early morning sounds, as the sun is rising. There is general excitement and camaraderie among the group of gathered Slaves on their day off. They are about to head out to the forest. Women Elders dressed in an assortment of bright red, blue, yellow and green colours, layered dresses with matching head ties and white lace-trimmed aprons; accompany the men.*

MALE ELDER 1 *(Chirpily rubbing his hands)* Marnin,' Marnin,' how you sleep, Mama Gang-Gang? You ready for de big Maroon today?

GANG-GANG SARAH *(Excitedly)* Eh-eh, Marnin,' Papa. Me, it was hard to sleep with all dis preparin', food to eat for de big day today. Everybody comin' together for a Maroon is a very big event and you could say is excited, ah excited so much; knowin' everyone comin', to help me, was too much to put me mind to sleep.

MALE ELDER 1 Eh heh! You know is glad I feelin' because we lettin' de young ones learn about what we see our fathers and mothers do so long ago. *(Shaking his head thoughtfully)* Takes me right back! Everytime we have a Maroon, it remindin' us how to always come together as one. Dis mission to help someone who has de most important need; puttin' a roof over yuh head, is what we have to teach de young ones. Dey will know dat one day, dey too will have to carry out de same practice, and den show others what to do, when it's their turn. After all, what else is dere for us to do?

GANG GANG SARAH *(Nodding thoughtfully in agreement)*
Yes, yes, you' right! I t'ank the Orishas first, and t'anks to all-you, comin' together to help me build me house today. I cook a big set of food and all de women inside dere, is busy cookin' all kind ah food too. So yes, you could say ah ready!

MALE ELDER 2 Mama, you don't have to t'ank us. Dat is what we have to do; it's de tradition we carry all de way from Africa inside our hearts. Dis Maroon – buildin' a complete house from scratch in one day for somebody, before de sun set, is what we learn from back home; a community with hearts showin' oneness; dat is how we must be, to rise as a people.

FEMALE ELDER 1 *(Joining the waiting group and addressing another female elder)* Marnin,' marnin,' how was yuh night? You sleep good?

FEMALE ELDER 2 Marnin' to you, Mama. Well, pain in de shoulder, lancin' me all night, but ah say, '*pain you have to go, you have no right inside me body*' and dat is how I'm here. So me, I carryin' de bell and de chalk to Papa Bois today!

MALE ELDER 1 *(Taking charge of the group)* Who have de silver coins and who have de rum for Papa Bois today?

YOUNG SLAVE I have de rum, coins and de bouquet of flowers and I think we have everythin' for Papa Bois; is not so it go?

MALE ELDER 1 *(Addressing the gathering)* Well yes chile, and it's time for us to go! De sun risin' and don't forget we have to build dat cabin before de sun sets. We need to make our feet long, long oh, and come back quick-quick!

GANG-GANG SARAH Isn't it good dat after all dese years in dis land, we don't forget what Africa teach us? Yes, it's good dat we honour Papa Bois, because as de Guardian of de forest, if we don' show respec' and appease him before we cut down his wood today, den we know dat trouble will be comin' to us for sure!

MALE ELDER 2 Where is Tom? What takin' him so long? We all ready to go and de day not waitin' for us; he mus' know, it just keeps rollin' along.

GANG-GANG SARAH *(Animated and relieved)* O look! He's comin' right now!
(Proudly she speaks in a soft whisper to another female)
Look at my bethroed, although dey beat him so bad over the years, he now have a bruck-foot, he's still a fine-looking man indeed! My very own childhood sweet-heart, after all dese years! And dere I was thinkin' he was dead, when de evil men raided our village back home, but look at dat, he end up right here; a slave, just like me, and on dis very Plantation too!
(Shaking her head and hands akimbo, she smiles proudly as she looks directly at Tom who's approaching them)
Isn't Olodurame good to me? To keep dis my Tom, safely all de way in dis strange land, for us to meet once more, right here! I think dat is no coincidence, it's Olodurame's decree!

TOM *(Quickly approaching the group and smiling widely)*
Marnin,' Marnin' all! Papa forgive me. Couldn' forget dis special axe! *(Grinning, he winks at Gang-Gang Sarah, then rubs the handle of the axe)*
Please forgive my lateness; I had to sharpen my special axe – dis special iron is for *Ogun*; it's very important for dis special job today. But, is ready, ah ready now; so leh we go! *(whispers to Gang-Gang)* A very special marnin,' to my sweetheart.
(The Elders lead the way to the forest. Tom clears his throat and leads the group in a song, from the back of the procession)

TOM *(Sings)* "By de rivers in de Caribbean!"
GROUP *(Responds)* "Where we sit down!"
TOM *(Sings)* "Dat's where we weep, remembering Africa!"
GROUP *(Responds)* "For de wicked carried us away in captivity; beat us to work with songs."

TOM (Sings) *"So now we're planting de motherland, in de Caribbean!"*
(*Reaching deep in the forest, the Senior Elder makes white Chalk marks on trees selected for cutting, as he prays. He pours rum on the ground in front of a tree: as a bell is rung*)

ELDER MALE 1 I come, Papa Bois, to offer by pourin' libation, with respect and honour, for all our ancestors, whose names we repeat now, and even de ones we don't know. I offer and libate their souls in de name of Olodurame. We call specially on Papa Bois, with a request to allow us to cut down some trees, for buildin' Gang-Gang a little cabin house.

ELDER MALE 2 (*Placing the bouquet of flowers: a bell is rung*)
Let dese flowers I now offer be a pardon for disturbin' your forest and all de souls dat restin' in it.

FEMALE ELDER (*Placing the coins infront of the tree: a bell is rung*)
Let dese coins, and flowers and rum serve as healin', by way of de Supreme Being on all spiritual levels, for those ancestors and spirits who were abused, afflicted, deceived, hated, and died brutally; as well as all who are still enslaved and constantly traumatised.

FEMALE ELDER (*Placing the lit candle in front of the tree: the bell is rung*)
Let dis light help to heal their souls. Let us, in takin' dese trees, escape from punishment and instead gain a protective shield from de shadows of despair dat we suffer here. T'ank you Papa Bois, for hearin' us!

ELDER MALE (*Addressing the group*)
Now we will cut down trees but rightfully, as we know, we only take what is needed to build a house; and not one tree more!
(*They cut down the trees they need for the house-building as they sing the call-and-response song again*)

TOM   *(Sings)*
"For the wicked carried us away in captivity; beat us to work with songs."

GROUP *(Responds)* "So now we're planting de motherland, in de Caribbean."

(The group return to the prepared area where they work animatedly, with urgency, they put the house together).

VOICE IN GROUP

Now, de house finish, it's time to celebrate. Look how quick we finish dis little place! Leh we dance and sing!
(There is drumming and dancing)

VOICE IN GROUP

Look, such a beautiful little house, eh! And see, no waste! Papa Bois is surely happy with us; look how quickly we finish too!

(Gang-Gang Sarah is ecstatic, she dances a celebratory dance in the middle of the group, with much merriment and camaraderie among them all; everyone joins in the celebration)

[Exeunt

ACT 5 SC. 3 – WEDDING & REBELLION PLANS

SETTING: *The men are sitting in a group by themselves, talking of an impending rebellion. There's talk of an uprising; led by a slave rebel called Jabari. He has been mobilising support in the neighbouring Plantations, with some measure of success. The women are discussing Gang-Gang's marriage to Tom and their preparations for the upcoming event.*

ANANCY So all-you hear there's a wedding in the air! Noh? Well, leh me tell you our great Mama Caribbean, Gang-Gang Sarah, is going to jump the broomstick with Tom. But hush, noh! It's a real secret eh, because slaves are forbidden to marry! Ssshhh!
I mean, you heard yourself, the same Peter Bristol, Plantation Owner, decree how slaves have to be treated. *(Moves closer to the audience)* And he calls himself a gentleman! Do gentlemen breed humans like animals; forcing men to sleep around with different, different women, like bulls servicing 2, 3, 4, 5 cows without stopping! What about their lives? No stability! No security! No family unit - definitely not like the Bristols!! No sir, that's not right! And what for? To make women breed children like rats and then he goes and sells them! *(Shakes her head disapprovingly)*
But if you're important to the Boss-man *financially*, like Gang-Gang Sarah is, you might be left alone to keep your children. Otherwise, by the time they turn 10 years old, they are wrenched from their mothers and serviced around the Plantation to work, until they become helpless little mothers too; just like their own mothers! What ah devilment! What ah everlasting crime!
(Shaking her head profusely)
As a woman, like me, you too would need to band your belly, *(Winces and writhes in pain)* – hurt – loss – pain. A-lot, a-lot ah breeding years, tired womb; body too tired for

anything else, until death say, *'Come home to rest!'* Believe me, that's how it goes. But……
> (A sudden change of mood)

But all-you cheer up, noh! It's Gang-Gang and Tom's big wedding day soon! I don't call it breaking any rule; let's just say, they're continuing with *our* own Motherland rules.

> *[Exit Anancy*

STAGE DIRECTION: *Curtain opens with two cameos – a group of men at one end of the stage and a group of elderly women at the other; changing spotlight on each group as their group converses. (Alternatively, could operate as 2 separate entries and exits)*

NENEN *(Discussing with a group of 3 women)* Dat wedding go bring a littl' bit of joy to all of us. Well, a'ready done start preparin' to make de broomstick for de ceremony. Ah tell you, it'll be de nicest littl' broomstick ever make on dis Plantation!

WOMAN And since we're not allowed to get married in dis strange country, it will be our very special hidden ceremony; takin' us back to a long time ago in another place; back-home in Africa.
(Nodding her head up and down)
The younger ones will see somethin' new for sure!

NENEN Ah gather all de broomcorn from de cornfield a'ready and ah have dem soakin' inside, getting' ready to plait de broomstick. And as soon as Edith could get away from dat Great House and bring me de string ah ask her for, ah go finish plaitin' de broom grass. We have just enough time – it finishing in jus' one day.

WOMAN What about the stick, you want me to bring a stick for you? Ah might even have one long enough to use as de handle. And as for de dress for Gang-Gang, who's sewing it?

NENEN Eh-eh! Is not me who is de oldest slave on dis Plantation, maybe 99 or more years old? Ah wouldn't really know and nobody here countin' years. Anyway, you should know dat de sewin' is taken care of too.
(Pointing to her cabin).
Ah have it right inside dere! But maybe you could get some children to pick nice, nice flowers, to make flower chains to decorate de broomstick. In fact, get dem to gather a good mixture of colours – like Alleanders: de yellow, pink and white ones would make a beautiful flower-chain to decorate de broomstick and also make a nice flowers-crown for our special Mama's head, too.

WOMAN *(Patting her on the shoulder)*
Thanks to you Nenen; You are a *real* Nenen for true; because that's what the name *Nenen* really mean; an adopted grandmother and mother to everyone on this Plantation over all the many years. We really appreciate you and all your efforts.

NENEN Chile, tanks eh! Ah seen too many troubles in dis place, an' one day soon, ah will be goin' home, when de spirits call me out from dis sufferin' land. But till den, we all happy to celebrate an' make joy for Mama Gang-Gang!

[Exeunt

STAGE DIRECTIONS: *(Men form a group on stage as they discuss the latest news)*

MALE 1 Well, as for me, ah say we must join with Jabari and his gang in the rebellion. It's bound to reach this Plantation soon. Everywhere there's talk of Plantation being burnt down and taken over by slaves. We're fed up on this Plantation too!

MALE 2 Man, ah hear they burn down the Plantation estate in Les Couteaux. It was only a matter of time; that owner was just too damn evil. Did you hear how he beat up and kill some of his slaves who try to organise a rebellion and run away? They get caught, so he get his Slave-drivers to give them a good hiding; an everlasting beating, until they piss and shit themselves, as they die right in front of everyone; all forced to watch in horror!

MALE 1 *(Screams of disbelief, with hand on head)*
Haaaaaa!! No Mercy? *(Biting his index finger)* Mogbe!

MALE 2 Yes, so it is and to make matters worse, he left their dead bodies hanging on trees for weeks, till john crow come everyday and pick at their dead fles. Day in, day out, in the hot sun, the stinking rotting bodies were left there to remind others of the consequences of rebelling and to also frighten would-be rebels; in case they thinking of doing the same.

MALE 1 Eh-eh! Wouldn't that make matters worse? The plain truth is, those who had to witness that everyday, knew that the spirits were not laid to rest. Then resentment grew hatred like a poison tree growing inside of them; until it spring roots and branches of hatred that eventually burst out in thunderous anger and outrage. This led to the slaves going on the rampage; killing, burning and destroying everything in sight, until the white master and his family and all their white Slave Managers had to escape death themselves. They abandoned the burning Plantation and made a run for their lives!

MALE 2 Well, ah hear Jabari the rebel leader, is going to meet with some slaves from this very Plantation, before Gang-Gang and Tom's marriage. As for me, ah intend to go to the meeting and hear what he have to say. We need liberating too! Those slaves who escape from Les Couteaux, ah hear they managing very well by themselves as they're free now!

MALE 1 Yes, not a damn person could catch them or say he own any one of them! They free now! All of them hiding deep inside the forest, where no white man can travel; not a single soul would find them there!

MALE 2 Well, that sounds like a pretty good result to me!

MALE 1 Ah hear they intend to live in the bush from now on. And maybe if everyone join in and do the same thing, we could drive out all Slave masters from every Plantation in this land! Jabari makes it clear when he says the reason we don't have our freedom, is because we don't fight for it!

MALE 2 Me, ah agree with what I hear he's been telling everyone: When you come to think of it, this is the plain facts - it's slaves who running the white man Plantation; working, planting, harvesting, packing, loading, accounting, even feeding the white man and his family. Jabari says we do everything very well but the one thing slaves don't get to do, is handle the money. The Plantation owner pockets everything from *our* hard work and leaves us with nothing; even the food we eat, we have to grow it ourselves, or we starve!

MALE 1 Look, there is enough men here on this Plantation, ready to follow Jabari and to take control; Jabari will give the command and advise us when to strike but we need to meet with him and his men. So, count me in with the rebellion! What about you? We have nothing to lose, and a lot to gain; which is a Plantation that we say is practically ours, and our freedom too!

MALE 2 OK, ah will pass the word on! You too can pass it on! At the same time, we must focus on supporting Tom, and do whatever is necesary to make his marriage celebration to Gang Gang the best we've ever experienced in this land.

MALE 1 So, we will meet here again, two days from now; pass the word on!

[Exeunt

ACT 5 SCENE 4 - DIVIDED LOYALTIES

SETTING: *The Kitchen in the Great House. Two House slaves are sat around a table discussing.*
STAG DIRECTION: *Ade and Edith, house slaves, are sitting in the kitchen, pondering what to do; given the rumoured doom of the Bristols' Plantation. They are in a quandry over their divided loyalties.*

EDITH OK, we have one hour to decide which side we're on – whether to leave this Plantation for good, and go with the rebellion, or stay with the Bristols. Think quick, before the Madam and her family come back home. So what you saying?

ADE Do you really care about what's going to happen to anybody in the coming rebellion?

EDITH Yes, a part of me say, you a slave, you have no right to warn white people about any rebellion. But another part of me say, only 2 weeks ago they baptised me in a river, to make me follow their Christian religion. Ah was thinking they must like us more than the field slaves.

ADE *(Shaking his head in agreement)* Mmm, I see.

EDITH Well, the point is, ah didn't see anyone else get baptised apart from us two. Maybe the Bristols not that bad to us. After all, they did say we're different now. What d'you think?

ADE Well, some part of me say, Ade, you a black man. All other field slaves outside this house, is black just like me, you should be with them! But then another part of me say, ah like hearing about what's in the white man's *talking* book. I'm always standing right in front of the Madam, when she read the *talking* book to those children – ah like those stories. And then to make matters better, they gone and baptise me just like their Christian Jesus!

EDITH Ah see whe' you coming from. And Mrs. Bristol say now we're *"clean in our hearts and the blackness inside us is washed as white as snow!"* Me, ah say don't know what snow is, but then she say to think of my heart being as white as milk inside now we are baptised!

ADE Look, at least as a House Slave, ah learn to read, by watching and listening to them read everyday, but at the same time, Ah pretend not to listen. Sometimes, ah secretly borrow their *Talking Book* and read it when no one is there. But this Bible book never seem to *'talk'* to me!

EDITH *(Laughs loudly)*
You really think a Bible book can talk! Maybe you're right eh. Ah don't know, it's true Mrs. Bristol is always saying, *'the good book say this'* and *'the good book say that.'* *(Laughs)* It probably really speaking to her then!

ADE Well, sometimes, ah don't really understand her. Ah wonder whether she might be doing some different kinda listening because I never hear that book talk to me! Maybe these white people have some special white magic to make their Bible book talk! In any case, ah done get enough beating from them to last me a life time; only because their book *say* as masters, they can beat me and that ah must always obey them. How the book could tell them that, ah don't know! But even so, when you weigh everything up eh, maybe ah still say they're not all that bad!

EDITH *(Stands, looking out of a window)*
That's what ah was thinking meself. Two weeks ago, when they gave us a special favour and baptised us in the river, what ah realise is that they're doing exactly the same thing as we did back home; when we worship our marine spirits in the running water. So if we smart, now we really can worship our ancestors in the water with them, while at the same time, believe in their Christian Jesus who

	baptised in water, just like us! Ah think that makes us different from the other Field Slaves - you don't think so?
ADE	Well, the Madam say, the blackness in our heart is gone, and as soon as we accept this Jesus, we have to stop believing in African gods, because they are all bad! So ah say to meself, this must mean we really are white inside us, since all darkness is gone in the baptism.
EDITH	*(Teasing him)* You mean, you think she saying you're white now? Hah! Well, my little bright eyes telling me ah can see you, a big black man standing in front of me! Definitely not white yet! *(She laughs out loudly)*
ADE	*(Smiles coyly)* C'um on, you know what ah mean. The Madam say now that we baptise, we are changed, and we mustn't go back to Gang-Gang Sarah's medicine or African belief in our Orishas.
EDITH	*(Sitting down)* Sometimes, ah don't know what to make of all their talk of their good Christian ways either. You see, there is something odd about all this desperation to baptise us so quickly; maybe they sense something! If you remember, it was the same Mrs. Bristol who pleaded and begged with us to go and fetch Gang-Gang Sarah with her medicine, to save their children. Didn't Gang-Gang give them black medicine to bring them back to life?
ADE	Yes, yes, you right! Did she say our black medicine was bad then? No! And she definitely *didn't* say it was dark then.
EDITH	That's true! ah didn't hear any talk about the colour of the medicine. But yes, she did plead and beg the both of us to go out in the middle of the night, to fetch Gang-Gang Sarah with African medicine; even when the Massah say not to!
ADE	So, what you saying?
EDITH	All ah could say is I'm confused. Still don't know which way to go.

ADE *(Standing)* The problem is this, when it comes down to choosing, ah have to think about meself. Ah getting old now. What can I do apart from this house work? Ah don't have to plant food to eat like the others; ah have a little space to sleep and my work is not in the hot sun. Furthermore, the Bristol children not as nasty to me now, as they were, when they were small. Now they're bigger, they show they need me more and now we are baptised, ah think we not real, real Africans any more. *(Shrugs his shoulders)*

EDITH *(Looking thoughtfully nodding)* Ah hear you! But look outside, the rain coming! Come, let's run and grab the clothes off the line, or everything will be soaking wet again. All ah can say is, soon, and very soon, time will tell.

[Exeunt

ACT 5 SCENE 5 – JABARI CALLS FOR REVOLUTION!

SETTING: *Deep in a field, beyond the Plantations, rebel slaves have gathered to hear from a self-styled rebel leader, Jabari.*
STAGE DIRECTIONS: *Flood-lit stage in white, trees in background. A mixed gender gathering is surrounded by the rebel leader in the middle.*

ANANCY: *(Singing)* 'What sweet in goat mouth, go turn sour in 'e bam-bam!'
Isn't that how this proverb goes? Well, you know what ah mean - the benefits are all the riches of the Plantations; all the slave live stock; all that resources from raping and pillaging of the land from people too weak to resist extraction of their natural wealth; will come to an *end!* *(Emphatically)*
All-you want me to say more? Just look at what you sit here witnessing - the loss of so many human lives; hunting, gathering, crossing the Atlantic sea with many dying in transition; fingering and prodding their naked bodies, mouth, even their †*bam-bam*; examining them like wild animals on auctioneers' public platform; breeding women with different-different men, to produce unbonded offspring; no family closeness and love, but wrenching litle girls away for servicing, or to sell as soon as their little breast seeds begin to show over hundreds of years, is a real abomination! A crime against humanity! A devilment! An evil! *Plimaliwel!
(Holds up his hand in indignation)

Notes: †***Bam-bam*** – Creole English word for your *bottom*
  ****pli maliwel*** – Creole French or *patois*, means,
    'I put a bad curse on you!'

Look, doh let me get vex now eh! All-you not stopping me? But, hear noh! I don't have to say much more because all-you been sitting right here all along; watching and witnessing how this story is unfolding.
And now we reach a major junction, a big crossroad; all-you have to listen *very* carefully, before you pass judgements. As for me, I staying in that corner, right over there, and I listening really, really well. *(With a serious tone)* Let the voices of the oppressed speak, before I pass my own judgements. What's *your* verdict's going to be eh?

[Exits

JABARI: *(Stands in a circle of gathered people in a secret location)* Brothers, and sisters, I stand boldly before you today because the time has come to claim our freedom! And let me remind you why you have a right to do just that. Look at us, our men, our women, our children forcefully taken away from our precious grasp; stripped away from our bosom mercilessly, cruelly; while you watch them weep and wail. You watch them as they are beaten till they bleed, their blood staining the dust before your very eyes.
CROWD *(Various noisy responses)*
Grunts!
Revenge!
Ah Legba!
We won't take it no more!
JABARI Yes, we watch them bleed and can't lend a helping hand. We watch helplessly, as our children are sold over and over again, to buy the very land you are standing on. These images are forever nightmares, dominating your nights that cause you to weep floods of tears that overwhelm your day. Yet, you are made to nurse the white devil's children with your own breast milk, and then he scorns and beats you, till you bleed. And that

shameless dog who calls on a Christian God, will say that your very sight sickens him; except when he openly, and shamelessly, rapes you women standing here. I say down with the white devil!

CROWD *(Clamorous yelling)* Down with the white devil!

JABARI *(Walking through the crowd)*
We plant the cane, we clear the fields, we plant more cane, we harvest the crops, we work the sugar mills, make molasses, make sugar; all with no gain. Look at yourselves - strong men and women! A wealth of talent is in this crowd, before me - a multitude of skills.
(Pointing to someone in the crowd)
You over there what's your skill?

CROWD Carpentry!

JABARI: And you here!

CROWD *(Various responses as he points to members of the crowd)*
Carving!
Blacksmith!
Driver!

JABARI *(Pointing as he walks among them)* Look, these women over there: they sew, plant, design, carve and the best carers you can find. You men over here, the best in building, farming – who taught you those skills?

CROWD No one!

JABARI Not even when they hide their books from us, yet our brilliance shows we have a head for mental accounting. But I'm telling you now, don't corporate any more!

CROWD No, we won't! No more listening!

JABARI Break your working tools and pretend not to understand their instructions! Create a go-slow on work! Defy all instructions! If you don't corporate, they won't have wealth from your blood, sweat and tears.

CROWD No more wealth! No more work!

JABARI And it's amazing how they mock us, saying we belong to them; the truth is, it is *they* who belong to *us;* as much as this ground also belongs to us.

CROWD That's right! This ground is ours!
JABARI You, me, all of us have a right to the land we're standing on.
(Walks through the crowd)
You women, how many tears have you cried, how many babies have you lost? Your bodies are tired from misuse and abuse.
(Pointing to an old woman, picks dust from the ground) You mama, over there, how many bodies have you buried in this dust?
(Groans and wails from the crowd)
JABARI *(Dashes the dust and holds his fist up, for silence)*
In other plantations many have even cut off their hands or legs and refuse to be any use to the white Plantation owners. You too need to use your Anancy-cunning and use your voodoo too! You can outwit the Plantation master. Why do you obey?
There are many slaves like you, who've refused to be slaves and they now enjoying their freedom; living in the mountains, where no white man can travel to. I've shown them the way and now I'm saying to you all, you too can have the same freedom.
CROWD Yes, We want the same freedom too! We want freedom!
JABARI You can live your life without the beatings, without anyone telling you what to do and without losing your loved ones on the auctioneer's platform.
(Walking through the crowd and pointing to men)
You men - you are not animal studs on a farm! Refuse to disrespect women's body to benefit the white man. Instead, you should be your own masters! We are standing on the very ground washed by our own people's blood. That's why it should stop now! So what do you want today?
CROWD Freedom!
JABARI When do you want it?
CROWD Now!

JABARI Yes! You have a right to this freedom. Today, is your freedom day! We are the capital, who feed their capitalism. And you and me we say, no more!
CROWD We say no more! No more! No more! No more!
JABARI Then, let today mark the end of the evil from the white devil. Let today be the end of his slave trade. Today, will put an end to him destroying us as a people.
CROWD Today is the end! Today is the end! End! End! End!
JABARI *(Yelling above the chants)* Victory will be ours, because he is weak – that's why to live, he must steal people from their own land and put them to work like animals. Let him go to work to earn his own keep!
CROWD He is a thief! He is weak!
JABARI He spilled the blood of our own men, women, and children, so that he and his family could eat good food and use us to build up his foreign homelands. But I say we put an end to him today. Brothers and sisters, what do you say?
CROWD End him today!
JABARI Today is your freedom day!
CROWD Yes, freedom is ours today!
JABARI And our victory will be taught to future generations. Our children and our children's children will learn how we fought the white devil, so they could be free. Use secret codes among you to out-wit and resist these Plantation Owners; without you they are nothing! They only have power because *you* are their power-base.
If you refuse to corporate, they will no longer have power!
JABARI Brothers and sisters, who is with me?
CROWD *(Loud, vibrant cheers from individuals)*
We are!
Yes, we with you!
Me too!
Ah ready right now!

JABARI So I say, let's burn him to the ground! His symbol of evil must fall down!

CROWD *(Loud frenzied chanting)*
Burn! Burn! Burn! - Burn! Burn! Burn!

JABARI *(Holds up his hand for quiet)*

Those who are elected as Advisors among you will take small groups and show them our prepared plan of attack. Follow this plan precisely. Listen to the chosen Leaders among you. They will tell you the meeting time and place of each attack. We will advance on the Plantations one by one; as we have done in a few areas already.

CROWD *(Loud cheers)* Yes, leh-we go now! Bravo!

JABARI *(Holds up his hand for quiet)*

Now remember, there will be many among us, who will be afraid to join our rebellion, don't be disheartened; their fear is also their great enemy. That's what you were taught to do, all your lives: to be afraid to take action and afraid of fighting back. But I give you my word; soon, you will all claim your freedom! Pass it on!

CROWD *(Loud frenzied, defiant chanting)*
Burn! Burn! Burn! - Burn! Burn! Burn!

[Exeunt

ACT 5 SCENE 6 – SECRET REBELLION PLANS

STAGE SETTING: *Gang-Gang Sarah is in her Cabin, where she is visited by various slaves for instructions on the plan of actions for rebellion on the Plantation.*
STAGE DIRECTIONS: *Soft lighting in Caribbean colours inside her cabin. Gang- Gang Sarah is seated in front of a small table, with an empty chair on the other side of her. There is a candle lit in the middle of the table.*

ANANCY And so it is, that much preparations have been made for the final battle for independence. Yes, resistance had taken many forms, maiming, infanticide, mutilation, poisoning, voodoo, murder and starvation to death but the coming rebellion is the mother of all resistance. This final show-down is going to be a furious battle of wills, to survive without oppression; as the free men and women they were from the beginning. Our mama Caribbean, Gang-Gang Sarah, is tasked as leader of spiritual preparation for their armageddon. Old people proverb say,*'when the cat's away, the mice will play!'* Ssshhh!

[*Exit*

GANG-GANG SARAH *(Addressing a group of women)*
OK, your training as warrior women over the years, I been teaching you will be put to the test in this rebellion. It will be a fight for survival, some of your it will be a fight to the death. But your combat skills and training have prepared you for this day. Every head of a group of militia warrior women will see me tonight for instructions of the battle plan. We cannot fail. We know that the Massah and his family are going to their overseas back-home, as they do every Christmas. This year will be their last! We'll make sure they won't be coming back here. This is our great opportunity to strengthen our efforts to keep him away. Jabari has plans for us to burn down and destroy this

plantation at Christmas. Yes, when the big fat cat is away, we, who he treats less than mice, we will make *our* play.

WOMAN IN CROWD Mama, may Legba bless and protec' Jabari and you too.

GANG-GANG SARAH I say Amen to that! The work we going to do will guarantee we take control of this Plantation and for the Massah to never return to this soil - together, we can make this happen! But to do that require a big, spiritual work. So we have to make special efforts to call on all the Orishas to help us. Remember, they came and helped us to cross the great ocean on the big slave ship. Believe me when I say, these Orishas will come and help us this time too.

WOMAN IN CROWD Ah ready mama, just say what the women must do, and I will organise them.

GANG-GANG SARAH OK, the very night when the Massah and his family drive off this Plantation for their holiday, we will be petitioning Shango, god of thunder and lightning, to deal with him. As you know, since they ban our drumming, we haven't been able to power-up and strengthen our prayers and petitions to the Orishas as we should. But tonight, we going to use every hidden drum on this Plantation to talk to the Orishas. Tell the others to get all their drums out every day: we need to do seven days of rituals.

WOMAN IN CROWD Where do you want us to meet for Shango ritual?

GANG-GANG SARAH Our first meeting place is at the Silk Cotton Tree. We must make our loudest requests known there. Bring some nails. Those Slave managers who like to drink the strong rum will not able to see or even hear us; they will be double drunk. We calling Gaunab on them. Warrior women soldiers will be on guard when they fall drunk. There will be permanent changes on this plantation, and no Slave owner will ever set foot on this Plantation soil again, after tonight.

WOMEN IN CROWD Yes mama!
That's great news!
What you want us to bring for Shango?

GANG-GANG SARAH Live animals, we will cook food to offer and speak to the Orishas, but in our own tongue. So tell the others to expect them to hear us when we connect in our own language. We meet one hour after the Massah leave the Great House.

WOMAN Yes, I will speak Yoruba, some will speak Twi, Ga, Fanti and more, it's how our spirits and ancestors know us. We must reconnect with them!

GANG GANG SARAH Yes, for the next seven days, we will refuse to speak in the white man language or answer to any name the Massah gave us; I will be just Gang-Gang. You tell everyone to revert back to their African names, so we can speak with genuine voices directly to our ancestors; that's how they will hear and recognise us.

WOMAN But Mama, Gaunab is god of death! You mean you're saying death to all those who steal us, take our identity and keep us here as slaves?

GANG-GANG SARAH Like Jabari, I'm saying, we take our freedom by force! We take control of our lives and we burn down the Great House at the end of our seven-day ritual. We will be masters of our own lives, just like the runaway slaves; living and managing by themselves in the mountains. So you must go now, because the men waiting outside need their instructions too. As you go out, ask them to come in.

WOMAN *(Curtesying)* Yes Mama, we need you. May Eshu guide and protec' you too.

[Exits

ENTER 3 men knocking on Gang-Gang's Cabin door

GROUP OF 3 MEN Mama we greet you, oh!

GANG-GANG SARAH My brothers, I greet you knowing there is a lot of work ahead to do. Thanks for coming. Our work must be swift, as we follow a strict plan, and fixed time to do all that's necessary.

MEN We know what will happen, we just waiting on the word. We were at the meeting with Jabari and consulted with the Planners for this Plantation. The word is, the day before Christmas, the freedom fighters from the Mountains will join with our men and women and we will burn this Plantation down and get rid of all Slave Handlers.

GANG-GANG SARAH OK, good. So we meet for the next 7 days to petition Shango in rituals for the success of our freedom. We must stick to the strict plan. Tell the rest of the men to refuse to speak in the white man's language and don't answer to any of the names Massah gave us; I too will be just Gang-Gang. You tell everyone to revert back to their African names, so we can speak directly to the ancestors; this way they will immediately recognise us. Our first meeting place is at the Silk Cotton Tree, one hour after the Massah drive off this Plantation for his holiday overseas. We must make our requests known on the first day of the ritual. Bring some nails.

MEN We really like the plan Mama. Thank you Mama.

GANG-GANG SARAH Get some men to join the women warriors as look-outs, and they will deal with all Slave Handlers when the time come.

MEN Yes Mama, we already organize them.

GANG-GANG SARAH Good, now go and succeed with the Orishas' help. As you go out, there should be Leaders of the Young mothers waiting outside my door. Please ask them to come in now. Right now, we have to plan swift and move swift.

MEN *(Bowing)* Yes, Mama! May Eshu be pleased too, oh!

[Exits

ENTER 2 young women knocking on Gang-Gang's Cabin door

YOUNG WOMEN *(Curtseying)* Mama we greet you, oh!

GANG GANG SARAH Greetings and thanks for coming. Now, this is your up-date; everything is well-planned for the day before Christmas rebellion. You need to know what you must do, just like the rest of us. Your job is to secure all the young women and children. The next 7 days rituals to Shango, will be outside in the bush. It will also mean that care has to be given to the young women, boys and girls, whilst we are away.

YOUNG WOMEN Yes, Mama we will do it!

GANG-GANG SARAH As Leaders for that group, your job is to keep the youth groups occupied with Anancy storytelling. Teach them their African names and do quizzes and questions on our religious beliefs. Speak in our African language, help them to enjoy their time with fun and laughter, whilst we cross over. There must be no fear, as we secure their future. Our drums will once again *talk* to our ancestors, so remind them of our pride in this. Their turn to drum will come on Christmas day; the day when we succeed in taking over this very Plantation. Go my daughters, it's getting late. Walk good.

YOUNG WOMEN *(Curtseying)* Yes Mama, thank you, we will do our jobs.

[Exeunt

ACT 5 SCENE 7 – CRY FREEDOM & THE BROOM-STICK!

STAGE SETTING: *The stage is flood-lit with vibrant Caribbean colours; drumming, music and a celebration is in full flow.*
STAGE DIRECTIONS: *It is Christmas day. Various groups enter the stage celebrating the success of the rebellion. All the Slaves are joyous, free and independent and are noisily displaying their happiness.*

JABARI Brothers and Sisters, welcome to a new dawn! A few days ago, what did you pray and work hard for?
GROUP Freedom!
JABARI And what do we have now?
GROUP Our freedom!
JABARI Yes! Long live our rebellion! You are free now! Those of you who want to join me with others in the mountains, you are free to do so. Some of you may want to remain here. There is no Massah here; there is no Great House here;and there is no sugar mill here either! Continue to plant and feed yourselves. Divide up portions of land, share among yourselves; live life as the free men and women you were destined to be!
GROUP Yes! Freedom!
We burn down *everything*!
We free now!
GANG-GANG SARAH We've been active in resistance and our war against slavery, in all kinda ways but today, we celebrate our success and mark this day as our freedom day!
GROUP Hooray! Christmas day! Our Freedom day!
GANG GANG SARAH From this day, let's practise your religion without fear, we will say our names without shame, we will speak our language too and remember the Anancy stories. They helped us to use our wit and cunning to fight back. Always remember that your culture is your identity.

It is what they tried to beat out of us, but we free now, to go back to all things Africa. Of course we will continue to develop new ways of living, right here in this Caribbean!
GROUP Long live the Caribbean! Where we free now!
GANG-GANG SARAH Let's return to what we are and what we know; as it was in the beginning we were a free people; that is how it is now, at the end of this rebellion; we're free!
JABARI Embrace your own freedom and let's help other slaves, languising in hell on other plantations; they too, deserve to be free. Today, the white devil Christmas day, is your Freedom day. Let us celebrate our victory over him!

There is dancing and singing and celebration. This is added to with Gang Gang and Tom's entrance. Gang-Gang Sarah and Tom hand-in-hand, lead the procession, with a large gathering of slaves following them, while others look on. They walk towards the two oldest Slaves on the Plantation, (Nenen and Old Joe), who stand waiting for them, underneath the decorated tree; armed with the marriage broomstick.

WEDDING SINGER *(Sings as the advancing couple walk up to the officiating Elders)*
Here they come, filled with pride and great resolve.
Hand in hand, reflecting unity in spirit and one love.
Witness their choice, we their well-wishers singing.
Women wearing best frocks and headties matching
In colours bright, near dignified men they all stand.
With best shirts and pants, clean feet and hands
Sealing practice that's ours, not forced - freely taken;
Honouring old traditions of ancestors we now awaken
Celebrate their love with time-honoured customs
Commit to each other, looking radiant as blossoms.
To you congratulations, we all sing as one!
To you congratulations, all singing as one!

OLD JOE *(Handing his stick to Nenen and taking the decorated broomstick from her: Gang-Gang Sarah and Tom stand in front of the Elder Slaves. He speaks to Gang-Gang and Tom)*
Now leh we pass dis broomstick over you' heads, to sweep away all de evil from you' new life together an' symbolise a new beginnin'. We doh need nobody to tell us *how* to marry one another because we have we own traditions; it goes back, back, way longer back, dan my 89 or is it 99 years?
(Scratching his head) In fact, ah doh really know how old I am, but anyway, who's countin' eh! *(There's laughter).*

NENEN *(Pointing to the decorated broomstick)*
Dis broomstick here has a deep-deep meanin'. Look at it, all of you, standin' in front me:
(Addressing Gang-Gang Sarah and Tom)
You two standin' here. What it sayin'? It's sayin' you're now connected with you' African roots; you' ancestors. Although you doh need a piece o' paper to say so, in we tradition says, dat is how you marry.

OLD JOE So now ah puttin' down dis broomstick right in front of us – me, your Ole Man Joe and dis 99 year ole Nenen here. *(Aside scratching his head)* Ah really doh know if she younger or older dan me, but *(winking at Nenen)* ah sayin' she look *real nice* today, eh! *(There's loud laughter then he addresses Gang-Gang Sarah and Tom)*
Anyway, right in front of us now, we goin' to witness you two jump over de broomstick with dignity, and in our tradition, we tell you dat you *are* legally married; as man an' his wife.
(The beautifully decorated broomstick is placed on the ground)

CROWD One, two, three, jump!
(Gang-Gang and Tom jump over the broomstick; everyone cheers)

STAGE DIRECTIONS:
- *There is much cheers and laughter and merriment, dancing and singing.*
- *Some women and men form a dance stage area and dance the Quadrille, mimicing the white Plantation Master and companions forms of dance, to much laughter and mockery.*
- *Kumina dancers, shown dominance in a competitive style to out-do the Quadrille dancers.*
- *Men with bottle and scrapers, take the stage space and some tamboo-bamboo are added in an old style of merry-making. The drumming and dancing and merriment continue well into the darkness.*

GANG-GANG SARAH Bring on the *Kumina* Dancers! Cement the African spirit in the Caribbean!
(Kumina dancers take centre stage, then move to the periphery of the stage).

WOMAN *(Enter Quadrille dancers)* Look at us, *Quadrille* dancers, we're not mocking the whiteman dance, but it sure can't compare with *Kumina* - no match at all - see how we're just walking and swaying.
(They move to the periphery of the stage).

MAN OK, stand aside, this dance has no energy. Now it's time for the *Kalinda*. It's what we created right here in the Caribbean. Plantation owners banned our talking drums but instead, we created the *tamboo bamboo* as drums.
(Kalinda dancers and tamboo bamboo drumming take centre stage)
Look at this fine piece of artwork, see how we dance the *Kalinda* with it? Bois! *(They dance in combative style, then move to the periphery of the stage).*

WOMAN Thanks to the *Shango* secret rituals in the woods, we still dancing today! Let us show you how Africa was hiding inside the Caribbean. *(Shango dancers take centre stage, then move to the periphery of the stage).*

JABARI *(Holding his hand up)* But my favourite is the *Devil* dance – Look at us, *Jab-Jab* and *Shortney,* man. We striking fear and intimidation, so we're *never* afraid. Keep looking out for us! *(They take centre stage, then move to the periphery of the stage).*

YOUNG GIRL And we, the youth, use our imagination to create new forms in the Caribbean, so we show you in our *carnival costumes.* That's why we will replicate it over and over again, and tell our stories every year on Carnival day. *(Young dancers in various carnival costumes take centre stage).*

You see, this way, we will never forget the seriousness of the circumstances that gave birth to our enjoyment; you see, we're not just dancing, we remembering too!

GANG-GANG SARAH So it is how, in this Caribbean, we mixed up our old and new cultures and customs. It is why whatever we look like, however we speak in this region, we could say:

EVERYONE *'All-ah-we-is-one!'*

Dancing and merrimaking continues, as each group exits the stage after their performance.

[Exeunt

EPILOGUE

ANANCY *(Enters in a jovial mood, laughing and dancing to calypso and pan music).*
Welcome back! E Kaaro o! Wha' happenin' deh people? Que passa? How you guys feeling now? So now you understand our story, eh!
(Anancy laughs out loudly)
So, I Anancy, have come to the end of my true '**Nancy** story! *(She laughs loudly).* Yes, it is our story. You see, when you destroy the sovereignty of a people, and you destroy their *name,* which is directly linked to their history, their culture, their psychological well-being; in fact, linked to their total cultural Identity, you must expect things to fall apart, before they restart! So, as it was in the beginning, look how they recaptured African spirituality, in the end!
It's just like our Queen of the Caribbean, Mama Gang-Gang. She lived a long and happy life, with her beloved Tom and their children. Some say when she died, she tried to fly back to Africa from a Silk Cotton tree; where they found her body. Some say she fell from the tree! Ah, but we know different now, dont we! *(She laughs and shakes her head)* That Gang-Gang, she's a true warrior woman, Caribbean Legend!

(She prances then stops, pauses, stamps her stick, points it at the crowd and shouts the traditional signal that storytime has ended).

ANANCY Now, all-you see my story's finished, so **CRICK!**
AUDIENCE *(The audience answers with gusto).* **CRACK!**
ANANCY The wire bend and so this story ends!
Steel pan playing calypso music

[Exit Anancy

END OF PLAY

GLOSSARY OF TERMS

1. A brief **Summary history of Trinidad** – the twin-island Republic began with the settlements of the Amerindian tribes, namely Caribs and Arawak peoples. This twin island was visited by Christopher Columbus on his 3rd voyage in 1498, which he claimed in the name of Spain. Trinidad remained under Spanish rule until 1797, but it was also settled by French colonists. Tobago, on the other hand, changed hands between the British, French, Dutch and Courlanders, but eventually ended up in British hands, following the second *Treaty of Paris* in 1814. In 1889, the two islands were incorporated into a single crown colony. Trinidad and Tobago obtained their independence from Britain in 1962 and became a Republic in 1976.
2. **Gang-Gang Sarah** was an African witch, who the folktales claim, was supposed to have flown from West Africa to Tobago, to look after her people spiritually - those who were taken to the Caribbean as Slaves, specifically in Tobago; Trinidad's sister-isle. She had supernatural powers like an obeah-man, was also a Plantation mid-wife and was known by everyone in the village where she lived. Legend states that she became the wife of someone called Tom, who she had known in West Africa, and had two children. Once slaves were freed, Legend states she tried to fly back to Africa but because she broke witchcraft rules about eating salt, so she lost her power to fly and fell from a silk cotton tree and died. This tree was believed to be sacred by African slaves who thought their ancestors lived in its branches. The silk cotton tree, which grows to over 200 feet tall, lives over 150 years. It is the largest on the island and it is well-known for the legends that are associated with it.
3. **Olodumare** (Yoruba: *O-lo-dù-ma-rè*) also known as *Ọlọrun* (Almighty) is the name given to one of the three manifestations of the Supreme God or Supreme

Being. Olodumare's name comes from the words ***Odu, Mare***, and ***Oni,*** which translates as ***"the owner of the source of creation"*** in the Yoruba pantheon. Olodumare is the Supreme Creator. He is god of peace, justice and tradition.

4. **Orishas,** (spelled ***òrìṣà*** in the Yoruba language and ***orichá or orixá*** in Latin America), are any of various spirits in West African (especially Yoruban) religious belief that can interact directly with human beings. These spirits are often invoked in rituals to influence human affairs or communicate messages from the spirit world. The term Orisha is also used in various black religious cults of South America and the Caribbean. The worship of Orishas has found their way to most of the New World because of the Atlantic slave trade. The practices of worshiping Orishas are varied and find expressions in rituals within *Santeria, Candomble,* around the Caribbean *Umbanda* and *Oyotunji* etc. The principle of worship is similar to those deities in the traditional religions of the Bini people of Edo Stae in Southern Nigeria and also the Ewe people of Benin. In fact, the multitude of names for some of the Orishas across the globe evidences the spread and synthesis of the original African practice with variations of expressions in the New World.

5. **Elegba or (*Papa Legba* in the Caribbean),** also referred to as ***Eleggua,*** or ***Elewa,*** is the king of the Eshus. It is the first and most important Orisha in Santeria. He is the owner of the crossroads and doors, who removes barriers and opens doors in this world. He is a spirit of communication and contact and who also witnesses a person's fate whilst acting as the connecting agent in this world. Elegba is often perceived as a trickster or impish child who tests our integrity.

6. **Ogún** is the god of iron, war and labour. He is the owner of all technology and because this technology shares in his nature, it is almost always used first for war. As Elegba

opens the roads, it is Ogún that clears the roads with his machete.
7. **Obatalá** is the kindly father of all the orishas and all humanity. He is also the owner of all heads and the mind.
8. **Oyá** is the ruler of the winds, the whirlwind and the gates of the cemetery.
9. **Oshún** rules over the waters of the world, the brooks, streams and rivers, embodying love, fertility. She also is the one that is most often approached for help in money matters.
10. **Yemayá** lives and rules over the seas and lakes. She also rules over maternity, as she is the Mother of All.
11. **Shango** - perhaps the most 'popular' of the orishas, rules over lightning, thunder, fire, the drums and dance. He is a warrior orisha with quick wits, quick temper and is the epitome of virility.
12. **Eshu** - the name Eshu varies around the world in rituals honouring these deities. Eshu, also called Exu (pronounced "Eshoo"), is not an Orisha, or Lwa, but are earthly guardians of the luminal, who are both a force of nature as well as spirits of the dead. In *Yorubaland*, Eshu is called *Èṣù- Elegba* and *Exu de Candomblé* in Candomble rituals. It is also referred to as *Echú* in Santeria and Latin America. In Haitian Voudou it is called *Legba* and *Leba* in Winti, as well as *Exu de Quimbanda* in Quimbanda, *Lubaniba* in Palo Mayombe and *Exu* in Latin America. Eshu is not a singular entity, but a class of spirits that are connected to cults of sorcery and necromancy from the Congo and Angola, that took root in Brazil, after slaves were brought over by the Portuguese, as well as around the English-Speaking (Anglophone) Caribbean.
13. **Obeah man** – A person who practices sorcery or witchcraft in the Caribbean. Such persons were known for casting spells or unleashing spiritual powers against their targeted victims or enemies.

14. **Basil the Devil** - He is a demon who resides in the silk cotton tree. Soucouyants have a pact with him to trade their victim's blood in exchange for evil powers.
15. **Maroon** – A term derived from **Spanish *Cimarron*,** meaning 'wild or unruly', refers to slaves in various parts of the Caribbean who, during slavery, ran away from slave plantations to create their own groups and communities as a strategy of resistance. Historically, these independent groups lived on the periphery of slave societies and were particularly prevalent in Brazil, Suriname, and Jamaica. In the context of this play, it refers to the practice of maroon society, e.g. the communal activity in challenging situations. This is shown by their autonomy, group strength, independence, self-determination, and self reliance. In the Eastern Caribbean, a large gang of workmen would voluntarily join forces to either plough a person's gardens during the planting season or assist in the moving and re-building of a house.
16. **Call and response** – (*in music*): a style of singing where there's a succession of 2 phrases; the first phrase is heard and the second responds to it, especially between speaker and audience/listener.
17. **The Great House** - There are many examples of the iconic Great House around the Caribbean. These houses were owned and built by Plantation owners during the 15th and 16th centuries, and in the height of the Slave Trade and plantation expansion in the region. They were occupied by the Plantation Sugar Barons, who built these luxurious mansions to ensure their comfortable lifestyles and protection on the Plantations, as they traded in sugar, cocoa, and later bananas in the Caribbean. These houses of grandeur were large and imposing, consisting, in some cases, of either ten or more bedrooms, a living room, a dining room surrounded by spacious lobbies. There were stairs which serviced the upper floors and a landing, with

white balustrades, and upper story rooms, surrounded by more lobbies. The size and height of these Great Houses meant they often overlooked much of the sugar plantation estates and many had uninterrupted views of the Caribbean Sea. In fact, some were adopted as forts with 3 feet thick of walls, to protect the Sugar Barons, their families and their burgeoning interests. Additionally, there was the sugar works, which included the sugar mill, boiling house and curing house, offices for the white overseers and clerks, who kept the plantation records, and storing for the processed sugar as well as rum. There were also trash houses for the dried cane, called *bagasse*, which was used as fuel in the boiling houses and stables; (with grooms who kept saddle horses for the masters and mistresses to ride), for the animals. Some Great houses even had hospitals, called "hothouses."

18. **Papa Bois -** In Caribbean Folktales, **Papa Bois,** also called **Maitre Bois**, is perhaps the most widely known of all our folklore characters. He is known by many names including "**Maître Bois**" (master of the woods) and "**Daddy Bouchon**" (hairy man). Papa Bois lives in the forest and he is the father or protector of the animals that live there. He is often seen by hunters and other people who live near the forest. He gets animals out of snares and treats sick animals at his dwelling. Papa Bois appears in many different forms: He is an old man who is very hairy, like an animal and usually is only dressed in a pair of ragged trousers with a bamboo horn hanging from his belt. He can turn himself into the form of a large deer or any other animal as well, to be able to observe the hunters unnoticed. When he takes the form of a human in old ragged clothes, he is hairy and incredibly old, or extremely strong and muscular, with cloven hoofs, and with leaves growing out of his beard. He is usually kind but can be dangerous when crossed. He might even cast a spell on a bad hunter and turn him into a wild hog.

As the Guardian of all the animals and the Custodian of the trees, he is known to sound a cow's horn to warn his friends of the approach of hunters. He does not tolerate killing for killing's sake, and the wanton destruction of the forest. He is known in some stories to appear to hunters as a deer that would lead men into the deep forest and then reveal his true shape, to warm them. He would then vanish, leaving the hunters lost, or on a quest to comply with some form of punishment. There are many stories of Papa Bois appearing to hunters. In the folktale there is some advice to the listener: If you should meet with Papa Bois, you must be very polite. You should greet him with,"**Bon jour, vieux Papa**" or "**Bon Matin, Maître**". If he pauses to pass the time with you, you should stay cool, and do not look at his feet!

19. **The tale of Anancy** is a direct transfer from West Africa to the Caribbean. It is the most popular of all the African folktales that were taken to the Caribbean via the slaves. The tales in West Africa originated from the Akan people of present day Ghana - *the original Akan name being Kwaku Ananse.* The name *Ananse* is an Ashanti word which means *"spider."* As an African folktale character, *Ananse* is a god in Akan folklore who can punish people for doing wrong. However, in the Caribbean or New World, (*e.g., West Indies, North America, South America, Netherlands Antilles, Curacao, Aruba, Bonaire*), the word *Ananse* was changed to *Anancy*; where he takes the form of a spider, which is depicted in many different ways. Being a typical trickster figure, sometimes he looks like an ordinary spider, and at other times Anancy is a spider which wears clothes or a spider with a human face. Overall, the Caribbean Anancy looks like a human with human characteristics but has spider legs. The character is also known as ***Ananci, Ananse, Anansi, Ananci Krokoko and Anancy*** in various Caribbean tales.

In Caribbean folklore, *Anancy* is a spider that acts and appears as a man, although he can adopt both male and female personas. For this reason, the character is popularly called **Compere Anancy, Nancy, Aunt Nancy, Sis' Nancy** or **Brer Nancy.** He is known for his quick-witted intelligence and appears to be able to make life enjoyable for himself, by outwitting others through trickery and fooling humans. As a trickster in Caribbean folklore, *Anancy's* portrayal also had a serious function; he operated, symbolically, as the intellect of the slaves who considered him to have the spirit of all knowledge. *Anancy* is said to have used his cunning to help them outwit their slave-masters; with strategies of resistance and clever ways of maintaining their identity. *Anancy's* trademark is using his knowledge of the ways that his victims think, in order to trick them and achieve his purpose.

20. **Kumina** - *Kumina* can be described as one of the most African religious expression in the Caribbean, (especially Jamaica), with its roots originating from the Congo region of Central Africa. In fact, this most African of expressions has stood the testof time and have survived the intrusion of Western culture via the Plantation system and post-slavery and independence epochs. *Kumina* rituals are usually associated with wakes, burials, or memorial services, but can be performed for a whole range of human experiences. *Kumina* rituals are used, for example, when help is needed to gain advantage over someone or something, such as winning a court case or for a lover. However, *Kumina* is sometimes viewed with suspicion as a form of witchcraft because of the trance-like state some of the participants, who fall into during the ceremonies. The original ritual is performed in a trance-like state, associated with drinking animals' blood for power, with some of the participants falling during the ceremonies. The ritual is characterized by ritual dance, spiritual healing, spirit possession, sacrificial offerings, spiritual powers, as

well as the celebration of ancestor powers. It is for these reasons *Kumina* is feared in certain circles. However, those who understand this religious expression, have spoken out against viewing *Kumina* as superstition, and against its misuse for bad purposes. *Kumina* rituals are led by men (called Kings) and women (called Queens). During a ritual/performance, both men and women can assume leadership of a Kumina sect. The men are called *'King' or 'Captain',* while the women are referred to as *'Queen' or 'Mother/Madda'*. The leaders must be able to control zombies or spirits and assume leadership after careful training in the feeding habits, ritual procedures, dances, rhythms, and songs of a variety of spirits, from their predecessor.

21. **Shango** – an identical African religious expression in the Caribbean, which is like *Kumina,* (especially in the smaller islands).

22. *Sangoma* Traditional healer, herbalist or witchdoctor. Sangomas are healers who it is believed can administer help through the ancestors. It is believed that ancestors from the spirit world can give instruction and advice to heal illness, social disharmony and spiritual difficulties. Sangomas work in a sacred healing hut or indumba, where they believe their ancestors reside.

23. **Ogun** – Ogun is the Warrior god of iron and war. He controls much of the material in the earth and represents primitive force and energy. He is known as ***Oggún*** in Cuba and ***Ogun Feraille*** in Haiti ("ferraille" means "iron"). The worship of Ogun may be traced back to Iron Age civilizations in Nigeria and adjacent countries.

24. **Damballah**, is a Vodoun god, in serpent form, who is supposed to have created the world and the gods, and is therefore the oldest of the gods. Damballah is said to be the most important of all the loas, who possesses the ability to communicate with and manipulate certain types of occult energies linked to curses and the underworld.

25. **Gamab** – Gamab is the Supreme God of Life, Death and Seasonal Renewal. Gamab lives in the sky and directs the fate of mankind.
26. **Gaunab** is the *god of evil and death*. He is enemies with Gamab, and Tsui-Goab. Gaunab created the Rainbow.
27. **Nenen** - A Creole word meaning Godmother.
28. *****pli maliwel** – (Creole French or *patois*), means, '*I put a bad curse on you!*'
29. **Doula** or Birth Attendant is someone who assists a woman in labour to deliver her baby. The word **"*doula*" derives from Greek,** meaning a *'helper'* or '*caregiver*'. Nowadays, it is used to describe a non-medical professional who provides emotional and physical support for mums-to-be during the process of giving birth. Sometimes this support continues into the postnatal period and long after delivery.
30. **The Yoruba Naming Ceremony** - called **Akosejaye** or **Esen'taye** – apart from deciding on what to call a child, is a process of determining the entire destiny of that child since it is believed that a child eventually lives out the meaning of his or her names.
31. **Babalawo** or priest of the Ile Ifá oracle. He is a trained and dedicated Ifa priest and diviner in the Yoruba community of Nigeria. In traditional society he is also a **"doctor",** a **"pharmacist,** a **"herbalist"** and someone who people consult for advice, guidance and medical treatment. At the naming ceremony *(Esen'taye),* the Babalawo is usually dressed in white and conducts the ceremony with beginning with a pray and introduction of the family to the guests and well wishers. According to Ile Ifa, the *Esen'taye* provides a family with a detailed analysis of the newborns' predestined character, moral strengths, ethical flaws, ambitions, major life transitions, and age-specific needs in an effort to avail parents of the best ways to raise the child in the midst of a volatile,

hyper-capitalist, and intolerant society. In addition, the psychological and sociological effect of Esen'taye on children is very, very positive due to the positive impacts of knowing the path to prosperity and success throughout various stages of one's life. *Esen'taye* is said to also give children a much-needed reservoir of self-esteem, self-respect, and dignity.

32. **The Agoji Warrior women -** The Agoji warrior women (the name originating from French) were commonly referred to as the Dahomey Amazons, from the kingdom of Dahomey. They were front-line army troops in the kingdom of Dahomey, an empire in West Africa which existed from 1625 to 1894. These women were not allowed to take part in any form of family life and were known to marry the King in a vow of celibacy. The job of being a warrior woman also provided an opportunity to move up in ranks e.g. gain positions of influence and command. The Agoji women were reputable fighters in slave raids, where they also took prisoners for the slave trade.

33. **Kalinda** with various spellings - *Calenda / Caleinda / Calinda / Corlinda / Kalenda / Kallinder*. In Trinidad Kalinda began as a combative stick-fighting ritual which transformed into a dance to the drum and shack-shack in the plantations during colonial times. The stick-fighting was characterised by stylized movements, performed by men (in some parts of the region, women also performed), wearing brightly colored costumes, dancing to dance-song that were sung by women. The dance is performed in a circle with two performers inside it at a time. As a form of entertainment, men in the 20th century had fun performing the dance using handkerchieves as pretend stick, when these were not available, to improvised tamboo-bamboo drums.

34. The practice of ***"jumping the broomstick"*** originates from Ghana, West Africa. The broom in Asante and other Akan

cultures also held spiritual value and symbolized sweeping away past wrongs or removing evil spirits. Brooms were waved over the heads of marrying couples to ward off spirits. However, couples often jumped over the broom at the end of the ceremony. During slavery, marriage between slaves was forbidden, and in defiance of this ruling, slaves took chances and declared their love by maintaining their traditional ritual, which is a declaration of public marriage, often done in secret.

35. ***Crick-crack* storytelling** - These African folk tale tradition is well known and practised within the Caribbean territories. Whilst some may vary in renditions, they are all variants from a common origin. One major characteristic in the storytelling is that it embodies performance. The 'Crick Crack' storytelling is a group performance in which the 'audience' participates in a close connection between the performer or storyteller and the audience. It presents an African format of a leader or storyteller and a chorus which is the audience, participating in a whole storytelling session.

    In other parts of the Caribbean e.g. St. Lucia, the storytelling is performed in French Creole or Patois and the Leader or Conteur, does a similar announcement that the story is about to be told, by calling out "Crick!" ("Kwik" in patois), to which the audience responds by shouting "Crack!"" or "Kwak!" Once the utterance "crick-crack" is completed, the Leader/Conteur continues by testing the audience with riddles, to which they would shout out the answers, in a session of exchanges. After this the story is told. The audience then becomes a chorus that is not only listening but also commenting. Often the riddles and exchanges are about their environment or what is known to them.

36. **Quadrille dance** - A quadrille is a type of dance for four couples, with each couple forming a single side of a square. This dance was developed from an earlier form of

square dance, and became popular in the French court of the early 19th century which was introduced to London society. An original version of this court dance would have been Ballroom characterised by its gracefulness and slow moements. The Quadrille was imported by European gentry who ran slave plantations, where the slaves would have witnessed and imitated the dance.

37. **Tamboo bamboo** is an ensemble made up of different lengths and sizes of bamboo which, simulated musical sounds of music; soprano, alto, tenor and bass. The Tamboo Bamboo involved pounding these carved bamboo sticks to the ground; a Caribbean tradition which originates from the carnival traditions. This skill was developed in Trinidad, after skinned drums were banned by the British government in 1884. However, Tamboo bamboo developed 'underground,' as a village activity, before being overtaken by the onslaught of new and popular metal instruments.

Proverbs in the Play

1. *If you put out cocoa, you must look for rain* (p47) – meaning if you've done something wrong, your guilt can make you seem more watchful of others. (Literally, cocoa beans which used to be put out in the sun to be dried, needed to be supervised in case it rained which would spoil the crop).

2. *Don't count your chicken before they're hatched* (p46) - don't make plans based on a good thing happening *before* it has actually happened, otherwise you might be greatly diasppointed.

3. *There's more than one way to skin a cat!* (p66) - There are several ways of doing something in order to achieve the same goal.

4. *Birds of a feather stick together* (p79) - Those with similar interests or of the same kind tend to form their

own groups. This proverb has been used since the 16th century.

5.   Teeth don't always laugh good things (p83) – It's not everything that you use your mouth (e.g.*teeth and tongue*) to laugh about is good.

6.   What sweet in goat mouth, go turn sour in 'e bam-bam! (p109 & p127) - When you find yourself doing something that feels good or pleasurable way, then having to face the dire consequences later. In other words, pleasure can turn into pain. This proverb was popularised by the Calypsonian **Seadley Joseph**, or better known as *"The Mighty Penguin"* or just *"Penguin."*

7.   When the cat's away, the mice will play (132) – people will behave as they like when a supervisor or other authority is absent.

Song – "Shosholoza"

+ ***Shosholoza,*** a Ndebele word spoken in Zimbabwe, is a dialect of Zulu. The word loosely translated in English, means go forward, move forward or forge ahead (with the idea of striving for something). It's an onomatopoeic, playing on the sounds a steam train makes, "shoo-shoo." With its origins in the hopes and despair of the early gold and diamond miners, **'Shosholoza'** is not just a song to South Africans, it is the country's unofficial national anthem and a hymn of unity and pride. Historically, South African miners used music to lift their spirits while working underground, often in trying and dangerous conditions.

Mixture of Ndebele & Zulu words	English Translation
(Call and Response)	*(Call and Response)*
Shosholoza *Kulezo ntaba*	Move forward (shoo-shoo) On those mountains,
Stimela siphume South Africa.	The steam train to South Africa.
Wen' uyabaleka *Kulezo ntaba* *Stimela siphume South Africa.*	You are running away On those mountains, The steam train to South Africa.

The former President of South Africa, Nelson Mandela, once described how he sang **'Shosholoza,'** as he worked during his imprisonment on Robben Island. Used in this play, the song underscores the depths of sorrow but also the prevailing unity in despair, division and the darkness of an unknown future; faced by the departing children.

Books by the Same Author:

- *Shakespeare for Children: Macbeth (2020)*
- *11+ English Preparation Tests for the CEM Exam (2020)*
- *Phonics & Spelling Workbook 1 (2020)*
- *Rhythms of Life: An Anthology of Modern Poetry (2019)*
- *Mastering Comprehension Skills (2019)*
- *The New Caribbean Folktales and Legends for the 21st Century (2018)*
- *Spelling & Word-power Skills Book I (2018)*
- *English Grammar: A Student's Companion (2018)*
- *Vocabulary Skills for Students & Teachers: A Practical Learning Toolkit (2018)*
- *A Woman of Destiny: A Calypso Novel (2015)*
- *A Woman of Destiny: The Text Study Guide (2015)*
- *T. A. Marryshow CBE – Honouring Caribbean Greats (2001)*

Phoenix Study Guides published by Eagle Publications

www.eaglepublications.org.uk

www.ingramcontent.com/pod-product-compliance
Lightning Source LLC
Chambersburg PA
CBHW041957080526
44588CB00021B/2774